I0533373

A Walk in
His Woods

Dimitrius A. DeMarco

DeMarco, Dimitrius - "A Walk in His Woods"

ISBN: 979-8-218-71757-5

Copyright © 2025 by Dimitrius DeMarco

All rights reserved.

No part of this publication may be reproduced,
distributed, or transmitted in any form or by any means,
including photocopying, recording, or other electronic
or mechanical methods, without the prior written
permission of the publisher, except as permitted by U.S.
copyright law. For permission requests, contact
Dimitrius DeMarco at dimitriusdemarco32@gmail.com

Paperback First edition 2025

For my family, both gifted and chosen.

"I taught you about Millay

and her childhood kingdom crumbling.

I spoke to you of Poe,

And his incessantly rampant rumblings.

Told you that Maya was the best…

But Frost was almost as good-

As you know, he wrote my favorite poem.

Together, we walked through his woods"

From "The Student (An Answer, a Digression)

By: Victoria A. DeMarco

Table of Contents

BRANCH ONE:
ARBORETUM

Black Oak

When my eyes eternally shut,
and my final words are spoken,
lay me far from the damned in their bitter graves,
where solemn stones lie cracked and broken.

When life becomes a mere memory,
and my final breath is taken,
plant me beneath the shaded wreath,
from a great dark black oak tree.

Let its brambles envelop me, mark me,
let it serve as my ultimate token.
Let its roots grow deep in winding ways,
marked with an arboreal headstone-umbral and oaken

Pine

Your heart is a seed planted upon your natural entrance.
Depending on your last stint, you will pay the price of penance.
Will you bloom robustly like a western Douglas fir?
Or will you be winter's bitter slave, forced to indefinitely endure?

I swear that I was born to be a lowly eastern pine,
indifferently aging like a cheap, generic wine.
But with a bold uprooting, I've been given another chance,
for in nutrient-dense grounds, one can change their circumstance.

This pine pines only now for the chance of reaching the pinnacle,
disregarding the drab and shunning the needlessly cynical,
ever chasing the possibility of a perfect and prosperous peak
to outgrow the birth-ground, where the nightmare's vehemently shriek.

Bonsai
Selective plucking,
perfectly sculpting bonsais.
Pulchritudinous!

Willow
Will willows wane
in whipping winter winds?
Or wax, weep, and wilt
in July's warmer weather?

Dogwood
A wooded crag grabbed,
ragged segments are peeled back.
Dogwoods still won't bark

Sycamore

New hands,
soft and pure to their very core.
Innocent and effervescent,
as deft legs carry babes-
ringing around the rosy trunk
of the young and sturdy
sycamore

Empty hands,
lost love in the name of ambition's pour-
Desdemona to Othello's Moor.
Honest Iago recites his
lies here too,
under the old and longing
sycamore

Greedy hands,
An ever-open door
insatiable in their envelopment,
like twisted branches
gnarled, snarling in the wind-
always seeking more
by the old and shifting
sycamore.

Desperate hands,
grasping at straws for-
being alive and alone
is a damning fate.
Sick of being less than more-
under the old and worried
sycamore.

Tired hands,
a voice that lost its roar-
surrendering what little is left
as the land collapses,
sinking more-
under the old and dying
sycamore.

Elm

Upon the green of summer's lease,
an elm tree stands with sturdy peace.
With boughs of leaves that shift and sway,
casting shadows atop the merry day.

A natural arch, a verdant dome,
a whispered welcome, a critter's home.
Its furrowed bark, a history told,
of seasons shifting, warm and cold.

A haven for the chattering bird,
whose joyful song is seldom heard.
Beneath its branches, lovers meet,
and children play with nimble feet.

Oh, noble elm, a graceful sight,
bathed in the sun's declining light-
a silent sentinel, grand and tall,
through summer's warmth and autumn's fall.

Though sickness comes and night may stall
the flow of laughter's gorgeous call-
the songs remain, a wondrous sign
of strength enduring in our time.

Sakura

In springtime-
just spring-
an opulent bloom
of Sakura blossoms
burst outward-
cherry red, the color of
lipstick and 7-11 ICEEs.

Dirt plots come alive-
vibrant and out of place,
surrounded by skyscrapers,
scaffolding, and the unsightly
patches of protruding pastel, (once)
now stained, blotches
of concrete and potholes.

To witness rarity in
full swing, juxtaposed
with hideous accouterments
is an eyesore that I find
undeserved, and not warranted.

For if it ought
to bloom for
merely a season,
let it be in a place
more worthy of its grace.

Cypress

It is in the nature
of water to take
the shape of its container-
even when said container
is a river floor-
sandy banks,
the winding roots
of cypress trees-
weaving their way along
the rocky bottom;
a wicker basket of
rocks and roots,
roots and rocks-
drenched in cool
and muddy waters.

Atop the surface, a
frog jumps frantically-
desperately from
lilypad to lilypad-
some robust-
some rotten-
all sunken and temporary-
as the cypress tops loom overhead
in the swampy world
of the mangroves.

Redwood

Redwood, redwood,
much better than some dead wood!
Hanging in a pile
of chopped up sullen logs...

Redwood, redwood,
still standing tall and proud wood!
With trunks that tower a mile
high and kiss the air and fog.

Redwood, redwood,
not bleeding out and slain wood!
For real estate and modern style
to pen the rich and fattened hogs.

Redwood, redwood,
eternally to stand wood!
Protect yourselves from mankind's guile
and the clamor of insatiable dogs.

Evergreen

Solemn seeds, sitting silent in sordid soils,
taking in inadequate nutrients.
Growing roots in deficient dirt lets no bud blossom,
killing all creation before it has the potential to ensue.
Ungrown pines bear no needles.

Frail flowers are not the only flora;
there is foliage that forests frozen fields.
Stoic stems and tense trunks, waxy coats on pin shaped leaves;
These keep them green all year, fine at all times.
Far less capricious than standard shrubs, don't you think?

Do evergreens remain ever green?
They live, they grow, but do they thrive?
Cold winds bring about hardened bark and unsweetened sap.
Are twisted branches and faded leaves just nature's cruel design?
Even still, it's all they've known.

So, what do you do when mother nature nurtures not?
How do you uproot tragic tendrils?
Is it far too late? Are those rotten roots far too deep?
The only way to find out is to start digging, but I have to wonder…
can you convince a conifer that it doesn't have to be cold?

Pitch Pine

Down towards the hollow's end,
past streetlamps and little libraries alike,
a bramble arch and gravel hill-
create a garden gate.
I stepped across the threshold,
the straits where the streets end,
and asphalt spans no further-
this is the place where the world begins.

It was as if I was visiting
a grand arboretum,
with a guided tour to boot,
and an education of what berries
were and were not fit
to introduce themselves to the tongues
of those who dared to roll the dice-
sweet? Or bitter?

Here, in a quiet clearing
roamed that rover, a metal arrow marking the spot.
They set up shop on a carpet of leaves...
Broken televisions and office chairs,
make up the crude facade.
A great controversy indeed,
just as the copy had foretold...
buried under the dampened soil.
You uncovered that, too.

I watched you reach into the brush,
unabashed, certain, unafraid in your natural extension.
You plucked a pin, placing it below my nostrils.
"Citrus," I said. It was unknown to me
that needles could smell like sunrise.
"It's called a pitch pine."
You could have told me it was Yggdrasil,
and I would have believed you.

A crabapple, blackened and dying,
sits in a field of rotting soy-
struck perfectly down the middle
by Jane and Rochester's lightning.
The trail thins, sand stands
where dirt once laid.
Shelving a cobbled overhang.
There stood a still'd pond,

10

overhung with dew and greenery,
where chloryphillic conversion
cloaks the view in serene firelight.

Beneath the meniscus,
two turtles snap outward,
drawn to beautiful reverberation,
rippling outward over the water's surface
as varied insects dance in tune.
You called them evil-
I called them curious.

We stepped away from the banks
of the stilled and stagnant reservoir.
My lips reserving words meant
for moments that never would manifest.
The dirt trail trudges indifferently...
onward and outward...

Through the quaint clearing-
a great divide divides in the brush,
and in that divergent looking glass...
the hollow begins anew.
the street comes into view...
That same damn streetlamp's glow-
you go left to your place...
and I turn right...
around and around in my circle.

BRANCH TWO:
DEDICATED DEDICATIONS

Snowy Evenings
- *After Robert Frost*

How rare now for scenarios like these-
where falling flakes waylay me in the woods.
Basking in the chill'd air of snowy evenings are
treasured instances – eternally lovely.
This is the ministry of the dark,
to stow all things sacred and
good. Frost piled high, burying deep
regrets and lamentations. But
were it destined that I
am to always unearth and have
interminably long looks at broken promises...
I wonder how I can be expected to
trudge upright, ankles deep and keep
my weary bones, mind and
feet from succumbing to the miles
laid out before me. To
rest my head and go
wander in darkest light before
hypothermic blankets entomb me as I
peacefully and eternally sleep.
Is that it? Is it just roads and
relics, vows and more miles?
No. I know that I am to
rise from this freezing grave and boldly go.
I'll be granted rest after, not before
I can answer when asked "who am I?"
Tis a lovely wood... but this is no place to sleep.

13

Two Thirds
- *After The Epic of Gilgamesh*

I.
Two thirds of you
liken gods -
and the other third
so fallibly human.

II.
You hold in your head
wisdom that takes a lifetime
to shape and cultivate
and still, you choose cruelty.

III.
Now all three parts of you-
god and human-
lie buried under shifting sands
and the broken walls of old Uruk.

A Carnival for Momus

Lions, tigers, lambs, innocence
in its purest form-
running amuck among the
tents and fiery rings,
trapeze acts and peanut stands
stared at longingly by elephants
standing on the heads of morons
and thrill seekers.

My father hated carnivals
but he loved the food-
and as he ate he would mock
the many attractions between bites...
pointed cap and
bells jingling with each
smack of the gums.

I raised my voice
to in some way protest-
to say that there is some degree
of showmanship, or even nobility
in the attractions brought by
strange people with strange professions.

He would say to me that:
"This is a carnival for Momus-
where entertainment comes
with the caveat of oddity,
and everything is done in jest."

I feel he fails to realize that perhaps he too
is a sarcastic god in his own right-
a God who can mock freely
the dregs and the denizens
with the expert lashes
of a cynical tongue.

An Aria in May

The new dawn brings
genesis, fresh harmonies
as the morning bell sings
and wind glides through fledgling trees.

New eyes will beam and glow
new hearts will beat and grow,
and the only terror in the night-
would be the cawing of a harmless crow.

For this aria in may
does as an aria may-
fill the spring air with song
as sprites go off to play.

And you, my would-be daughter,
my most beautiful, perfect song,
though the mornings grow tired and hotter
I'll love you as much as the day is long.

Metallurgy
- *For R.B.M Jr.*

Metal men, molding, forging
more metal men:
gold-toothed, steel-toed or silver tongued.
hollow men, tin men, iron men,
brass men dilapidated and rusting
reliving an aluminum illusion -
"rub some dirt on it."

Metal men mind melding,
"just change out the parts..."
Metal men now welding
new limbs, new cocks, new hearts (not beating)
compensating with their compensation
not comprehending that
vanity is perpetuated by metallurgy
strapped onto the necks and wrists
of a metal men militia-
MARCH! In the streets...
MARCH! Down the runways...
MARCH! Towards an early grave.

How it Shines
- *After Andrew Hozier-Byrne*

Something you ought to know, darling
is the cold unfortunate truth. There's
now been far too many a
time where an aching part
of my foolish-heart, of
my unresting head, of me-

that's stuck in time. I'm
caught between lives, afraid
that never will
I be granted relief. Always
condemned to be

tortured and trapped-
tongue butchered and silent within
ropes and bondage, an
image from a terrifying abstract-
a prospect from
the deepest recess of a
mind reduced to a single moment.
The blackest darkness in
the deepest pitfalls that my
hopes deem to be "light" and "life."

But they grow and linger unabashedly like weeds
worming their way up, up
and outward, out through:
the cracks in my speech, the crevices, the
spaces and places I thought were solid concrete.

Watch, chew nails as the surrounding traffic
whizzes by, no turn signals- picking
no lane until the road winds up
and out of view at light speed.

Any and all
semblance of my
self-love, self-hatred, your love
Dear, and the words you say, and
the promises you make fill me with a terror
that seesaws and teeters, un-balanced
as fear, in a deluge spills there -
into the streets between

the cracked and broken slabs... and those
wonderful pair of brownstone eyes.

But baby, I need you to really see
through your glistening tears how
much that I am yours, that I'm in "it-"
but a moment that isn't yours still shines

in these pupils of mine. I still see
it some nights in dreams, remembering how
these fragments scatter along the floor- and how it
too, under the light of a scarlet moon... shines.

Ghosts
- After Stephen King

Silent eruption, he
swings and thrusts
wildly outward his
hands in balled fists...
crashing up against
solid wood and the
cold facades of fence posts,
creaking, splintering and
yet standing ever still.
His hands are fine, he insists...
crimson lakes pool on concrete as he
gazes upward and again sees
specters made of moonlight, or the
horrors that we call ghosts.

Ode to a Grave Robber

Every moonlit night,
when the stars hide and
even the ghosts dare not
come out into the chill'd eve-
a sallow man, pale and sickly
with sinkholes for cheeks,
a ghastly gait,
corroded teeth and a gaunt expression-
limps out with his shovel cane
and digs up the dirt
at his place of choosing.

Atop the plot
he grips his spade
with the kind of strength that
could not come from a man
of such a stature-
each phalange holding strong
with the force and vigor
of the young man he never was.

He takes, like a thief
from their place of rest
a set of old memories-
now decayed and rotting (full rigor)
and holds them to his chest
clasping harder than he had done before
on the staff of his nefarious tool.

This man, this thing,
this grave robber and necrophiliac
for lost things he never had
lives a waking death that pulls him closer to the
very graves he stands above...
and soils the soil that sits below.

Ode to Daedalus

It was not so long ago,
that in your hay day…
you constructed Cretian mazes for crown'd kings;
imprisoned minotaurs, and crafted grand bovine statues,
that landed you in the graces of the ones they deemed nobility.
You raised their masts and sewed their sails,
manufactured saws, axes, glues and all manner of carpentry.
It was in the eyes of your sculptures,
that King Minos and his bride found your use…
they claimed you for themselves.

They locked you in a blackstone tower,
the design was crude and the material brutish,
shoddy bricklaying, splintered floors, and rusted bars-
laid the detestable foundation on which you'd give in…
capitulation in its most despondent form.
I watched your might, your mirth, your vibrance…
fade to toils and bitter silence.
You plunged your head into laborious sands…
only the ramblings of a maddened mind could be heard…
The echoing whispers of ghosts banging against the walls of their mad
machine.

You stared desperately, day in day out,
watching the sill for your next moment of hope,
your cerulean eyes filled with the interminable horizon.
And those moments of hope came…
and came again… and again after that.
For you would charge the perch
with Hermean swiftness,
lacing your fatigued fingers firmly
around unsuspecting fowls,
gulls, pigeons, squabs,
or any feathered beast that dare seek respite-
pluck their feathers and eat their hearts,
and I watched as your every waking moment
was consumed with thoughts of flight.

But your consumption
only decreased your appetite,
and though you were starving
you did not hunger.
Still, you slapped together
the means of our escape-

21

and together we jumped from
our birdcage out into the open world...
and then I felt it.

The heat, the flame, the holy fire,
would lift my wings and then inspire-
a lifetime lived in the light's embrace...
or a blaze of glory never before seen
by the likes of your kind.

You said to me...
"Son, do not soar so close to the wretched sun...
it will singe your feathers and melt your wax...
and send you spiraling into an indifferent abyss
where not even the light could reach you."

I said to him...
"These wings are not to wet-
to be soaked with the foam
of the vicious sea below us!
You grow so concerned from the sun,
but neglect the waves from flying too low!"
"If I am to die!
If I am to expire!
Let it be in burning glory,
with the courage to soar-
rather than be struck down and marred
by an indifferent world-
or the sands and shoddy floors
that you have grown so accustomed to!"

"Fly!
Fly with me!
Even if you die!
Fly for one meager moment!

Prove
     to
         me
            that
                you're
                    still
                       alive!
                          ..."

Pufferfish
- For E.H.D

Sometimes I picture you
trapped inside of a moment
that you could not help being in.
The sun rises.
The tides roll.
The bus comes everyday-
at the same... exact... time...

Sometimes I picture you
trapped inside of that moment-
with your chest stuck out,
your shoulders raised,
your spines primed and at the ready,
laced with the same poison
that lines your lashing tongue.

Sometimes I picture you
fighting in that moment,
pufferfish filling my mind
as air fills your lungs,
and fills your body-
and what leaves is a voice
that comes from outside of you...
as if you were being strangled
by winds and by cruel circumstance.

I picture you
in a moment merely talking with a voice:
a voice deep,
a voice masculine,
the humor of Twain,
the subject matter of a sportscaster.
A disposition that isn't yours-
but it has to be to ensure survival.

I pray for you
as his eyes present to him a "woman..."
as his eyes present to him a target.
But your voice is strong-
your chest is strong-
your shoulders strong-
you present to him strong...
and he loses interest,

mistaking you for something
you shouldn't have to be.

I picture you both
stepping onto the blue platform
of the dilapidated SEPTA bus.
He walks in, sits in the handicapped spot.
You march toward the back,
step up, remove your bag,
hug it tightly,
and deflate.

Glass
- For W. "J." L

You are a glass man...
in a glass house...
in a glass borough...
bring on the stones.

Amethyst Atmosphere
- *For L.R*

Syzygy breaks that hazy lilac sphere,
stars fade and fizzle, a thousand long goodbyes,
admiring an amethyst atmosphere.

Crashing comets bring vicious violet fear,
false promises and gorgeous golden lies.
Syzygy breaks that hazy lilac sphere.

Novas erupt and burnish all that's near,
you could watch with me as that bleak star dies,
admiring an amethyst atmosphere.

Lunar light lines your luminary tear,
and like moon tides, azure eyes swell and rise.
Syzygy breaks that hazy lilac sphere.

Eclipses mask a much brighter frontier.
Landscapes you'd paint with lush lavender dyes,
admiring an amethyst atmosphere.

Cruel constellations crumble when you're near,
magnitude matters not under orchid skies.
Syzygy breaks that hazy lilac sphere,
admiring an amethyst atmosphere.

Begging Morpheus
- *For an insomniac*

Shuffling, shifting, restlessly floating...
in the weightless awareness of your own gravity-
open orbit in the dead space of your bedroom.
Sanguine streaks across dilated pupils...
crimson crags, a maroon monsoon-
over white sand sclerae.

"Your eyes are blood moons,"
he spoke, with eyes staring softly into yours.
Ceruleans of his own...
the stare of a thousand oceans, with a subtle isolation-
matched only by Nemo's point.

You say to him:
"Sleep, my dear...
is for those who wave their white flags...
in sweet surrender...
and I, in my inflicted mulishness,
am not capable of such capitulation."

You leave the room,
and allow him to rest-
in this hall of your creation...
where he shall soon, unlike you,
be greeted and knighted-
by the one they call the dream king.

You departed in your clouded chariot,
and trudge towards your nightly war.
You place your book and cigarettes-
upon the sill, moving the ashtray just so...
until the words run out,
and the carton is empty again.

It is only after those fleeting pleasures deplete,
and the last of your escape is supped...
that you lower your knees to the ground,
clasp your hands atop the sill-
in ecclesiastical formation...
your ritual, biblical as ever,
finds you praying to gods new and old,
plausible and outrageous-
death bringers and heralds of light alike.

You pray for the deletion of consciousness,
like TV static fading-
after ripping the cord out of the wall.
You pray for your head to hit the hardwood floor like cement...
for even the rigidity of concrete slabs-
would be a velvet ocean,
the meniscus wrapping its arms
around your head as you break its surface-
and begin to drift...

but no drifting ever occurs,
and so you plead.
You stare into medicine cabinets,
begging pill bottles,
begging melatonin,
begging morphine,
begging any machination of a mind more morbid...
to grant you permanent immunity-to the toils of an insomniac's ill.
To be gifted any rest...
any closing of the eyes...
any unconscious bliss in pureness you've surmised...

You find yourself-
begging Morpheus...
a defeated plea leaves your parted lips-
as sun rays usurp the starlight...
and your arms fall into place-
neatly by your side.

Your body has reached its earthly limit,
your mind is forced to wander...
in the worlds of light unseen-
in our wakeful state.
But, this result you sought...
was not the work...
of devotion nor prayer,
nor begging Morpheus.

The Things That Darkness Brings
- For J.T (After Lord Huron)

Some nights, I don't know how to say this- but, oh

27

well, here goes something or other. You
make me feel like the world's greatest fool
for never knowing that there
are worlds beyond ours, there are
the kinds of games with kinds of rules
that I never knew existed. I
want them to play them all. Am
I okay? Is the light at the end a train coming
through the tunnel, barreling down the tracks, eager for
me to be put back in the dark- is that you?

No. There *are* a second set of things that come with darkness...
quiet nights, bright stars, and that brings
both the righteous and the evil
out into the air, a blend of all things
that cut the skin and yet nestle in my chest. Oh,
how wrong I have been about darkness... for
one world ends in a reckoning-
and a new one begins

Ode to Lethe

I often bathe in the
glorified and hyperbolized
highlight reels and montages-
collages of catastrophes and
joyous memories all at once
as each flashback shatters
any semblance of classical unities-
though there is one correction to be made...
I mostly drown in them.

I wish to be led to water,
to be taken by a guide-
be it Virgil or Vishnu or Tenzing Norgay...
I don't particularly care at this point.

I seek the end to my suffering,
I do not seek a fountain of eternal youth,
or the secret to immortality-
but rather I desire
to soak in Lethe and
forget what I ever wished for
in the first place-

and be one who has
forgotten what I've forgotten-
as it has been more than most
will ever know.

1960's Television

When I was a boy growing up
on the high sea straits
of C street, Feltonville, Philadelphia-
I saw the world within the confines
of a segregated abstract image
produced by the ultraviolets permeating
from the screen of a 1960's television.

Color was not a factor yet.
My best friend Da'jon was just that-
my best friend.
My titi Janet and her kids were more family to me
than the snakes with which I share blood-
for mine runs hot, and theirs chilled.
My brother Saul was not my half brother,
not half black,
nor half white-
he was just the kid who introduced me
to a little club called mock trial.

My grandmama Harlana Freeman
taught me more about soul and food
than the coal and crude
that my "Mom-Mom" served me on
overpriced plates with meals
that she had catered.

It was a black woman,
who got me to eat brussel sprouts for the first time-
she used bacon and garlic.
It was a black woman who encouraged me
the first time I found myself lost on a stage
reading poetry just like this.
She is in every room when I perform.
It was a black man who said I should write this poem,
thank you Jaylen.

At some point the dial shifted, the lights changed,
the parts in the tv were swapped out and replaced,
producing a new kind of image.
It was like the world had a sign over it
that read out boldly
NOW. IN. COLOR.

Many have taken this image and distorted it-
told me how to think or feel,
told us all how to do so.
But I have learned from love and time,
that color is not a binary item
to be used and politicized.
It is not a dual of consciousness
that W.E.B DuBois feared,
nor a weapon of social destruction.

Color is to be a celebration,
a holiday in which flags fly and are waved-
waved in beautiful surrender.
That flag likens a tapestry,
the sewing and hemming done by hands-
paving a way for a farewell to arms.
That sewing was done by hands,
hands worn, hands torn,
hands- just hands.

That surrender is not one done from weakness.
It is the correct capitulation of conscientious objectors-
deflectors, deflecting bullets meant for:
my mentor,
my best friends,
my brother,
my grandmama.

This world is NOT an abstract image
plucked from the picture produced
by a 1960's television.
The color is more visible,
more loud, more vibrant and vivid
then it has ever been allowed to be.
And, though it is different from mine,
it is a similar canvas…
a canvas to be painted with the same 1080p paintings.

Color blindness is a disease-
or a choice,
it's been sixty four years to date-
buy a plasma screen.

Name
- For my father

I wear my father's name
in the same bashful way
that he does.
Because he knows
and I know,
that it is not entirely his.
It was given to him
by his father,
and his father's father before him-
one was spineless,
the other, abusive.
But my father,
in his quiet way,
broke his own cycles.
No matter how much
I loathe the nomenclature:
my father's name,
my father's life,
my father's sacrifice-
my father is the sole reason
that I haven't changed it.

Still Waters
- For my aunt

Still, even after all these years your
waters rage in a serene river, one that will
run long after you have kissed the moon that reflects back in
deep pools and gleaming lakes.

Your Light
- *For my mother*

She would dawn her favorite sundress,
cloak her hands in white gloves
and kneel before a garden bed-
just there in front of the ruby brick wall.
Trowel in hand, she'd paint-
paint her white gloves, white dress and white skin-
with earth and sun,
darker hues on a perfect canvas.

It was in said garden
that I was planted.
Surrounded by homely warmth,
a mere glint off her visage,
perfect photosynthesis.

She loved me the way
fables told us of.
The kind that both oppressed and uplifted-
without discrimination.
A towering aegis that stood between
monsters that Lovecraft conjured-
and lawful matriarchs,
shrouded under the haunting guise
of something grand.
Though I'd be willing to wager,
Lovecraft would approve
of that particular brand of malevolence.

She "protected" me the way
Jacob Grimm warned us of.
Tying me to that gardens wall,
the vines and bramble twisted...
warping, nearly breaking.
But I didn't. I couldn't.
I asked her to let me go,
and with reluctant hands, she did.
So I grew and have her to thank.

So, to you, as if under sacred oath-
I vow, I pledge, I swear, I promise.
You who tamed vehement beasts...
you who rose vivid rosebuds,
and vibrant hydrangea bushes alike.

33

Be it at dawn's bright break...
or nightfall's sable brink-
be it under direct shine,
or vicarious gleam...

The world will know your light

BRANCH THREE:
"ALL THAT FALLS"
– Between the Cracks -

Anchor

Long have I been sat here, long have I had to wait
longer still has it been since my arms and crown were cleaned.
Once a year do I see the sea, only once I take the plunge
for I am me, but what am I?
Ah yes, I'm just a weight.

This place I lay, these walls I see, these walls I call my home,
this tawdry skiff of oak and pine, I exist here all alone...
Till once this year a thing did come, one with arms like me,
a brave old thing, that year after year, dared to go to sea.
This vessel had ventured many voyages,
this boat was battered and bruised,
but out again like clockwork, this humble craft did cruise.

Despite the cracks, despite the waves, the ship remained afloat,
and somehow still, after all these years, smoothly did she sail.
With a mighty heave and hefty ho, the man did throw me o'er,
sunk I did and cool was the sea below the wooden boat.

But from land afar and shores unknown,
the whipping winds did rise...
a storm so harsh and waves so rough
with foamy swelling tides.
Thunder roared and lightning cracked
in the blackened daytime sky,
but there below I could do naught, for Anchors cannot fly......

Desperately, the chain that bound me
wearily clasped and clung,
but the iron was worn and the links had torn,
and that chain was all but wrung.

The storm had stopped, the seas has calmed,
yet nowhere to be seen-
was hide nor hair, mast nor sail,
in the place that boat had been.

The place I'd lay, the walls I saw,
those walls I called my home...
lives only now in fond remembrance-
below the ocean foam.

Tomorrow

There's time that I've relinquished,
so while I'm here, I'd ought to speak, ergo-
say the words, you'd planned ahead...
but I can't, no matter how many phrases I borrow.

For I have felt no greater anguish...
I have known no greater sorrow...
when all the things that I should have said,
came to me tomorrow.

War

Be you a gladiator-
or utilitarian philosopher,
masquerading as a king or a prophet-
know this, and know it well:

Regardless of the victors,
and the boon of spoils-
or the circumstance,
and earthly consequence...

the war waged
will rage on eternally,
for there will always be
another battle to fight.

37

Unfinished Concerts

The music plays,
the dancing starts-
the rhythm matches
your movement as the world
exists in a twelve square-foot
patch of grass, centered
right in front of a Skyline stage.

But in the distance there is thunder,
and the rain starts to pour
over the uncovered, outdoor
venue, hundreds filing -no,
running, racing out towards
the cover of their cars-
not even halfway through the setlist
of the opening band.

In that moment I lost you,
or perhaps you lost me.
These days that memory gets diminished,
just like leaving that concert
before it was finished.

Wasteland

Words are an endless wasteland,
many miles of golden, grainy sand,
where in the dunes do the metaphors meld?
Where in the caverns do the analogies amalgamate?
Desert winds weathered by those who dare to compare,
racking brains and feet alike in a pointless odyssey.
I wonder if pointless is the right word...

We stumble, treading upon the tracks of
those that trekked before.
We extemporize and plagiarize
in the pursuit of circumventing the trite and tattered,
it seems impossible for everything
to be compared to everything, but-
it seems our life's bell will chime
before that particular horizon is reached.

Hell's Astronomers

Our world's most magnificent yet
simultaneously morbid and maddened minds
pass through Dante's Mephistophelian gate to Nessus-
where doomed souls stay sequestered.
Observing from a magma laden hellscape,
be it Galileo's gaunt ghast or Socrates' specter-
craning permeable necks, impervious to the ache...
staring arduously upward (there is no below.)

Do hell's astronomers look up and call us stars?
Or are we merely fleshy collages of carbon and calcium?
Homogenous mirages of hydrogen bonds?
Or through ruby eyes, through a brimstone telescope-
Do we mirror supernovas?
Do we brand black retinas with blinding radiance?
Do we silently smolder?
Do we shine with dazzling wonder through the eyes of the demonic?

Do hell's astronomers look up and call us stars?

Farewell

I pay this fare to the fair wishing well,
a penny I found, lying at the pauper's feet.
I thumb the coin, and throw it well,
I bid farewell to the fare I found
there by the pauper's shoe.

The fare broke the fair well water's surface,
rippled, twirled, and sank.
It rested there at the fair well's bottom,
bidding farewell to the light,
and the comfort of my hand.
Copper would not fare well in this fair well.

I wished at the fair well,
the reward of my fare, well-
I do not fare well when saying farewell,
even to my fair fare, in the fair well.
I wished at the fair well,
to never need another "farewell"

"One more," the fair well whispered.
"One more that you must bid,
Leave me, leave your fare, go, farewell!"

So fare thee well to the fare I found,
the fare at the pauper's feet, now,
The fare in the fair wishing well.
I wish you well,
fare in the fair well.
I give to you my final "farewell..."

Final Hour

Regardless of your strength and power
the reaper is a foe no soul can beat.
The bell will ring in that final hour.

You wear his name like stolen valor
in boots that will never fit your small feet
regardless of your "strength" or "power."

So to you, my kin, with blood so sour,
achievement is such an unsavory sweet,
for the bell will ring in your final hour.

Yes, even the bravest will hide and cower,
when life's brief candle loses all its heat,
regardless of your strength and power.

Your fleeting reign, a wilting flower,
will crumble fast, a bitter, grim defeat,
the bell will ring in that final hour.

So cease your boasts, your endless glower,
and face the truth: all lives meet their replete,
regardless of your strength and power,
the bell will ring in that final hour.

I Know

I know firsthand
the difference a day can make.
Differences paying dividend,
moments molded, multiplied and amplified,
culminating into a compiled crescendo-
then collides in a harmonic convergence
from the grief engraved in you
like an emblem on your chest
carved from his might and her light.

You are the concoction crafted
from everything that you know,
everything you don't,
everything you know that you don't know,
and everything that you will.

You are more
than you will ever know...
trust me,
I know.

Stargazing in a Cloudy Sky

A dirt trails ends,
a rare sight to see-
for it was paved by hand.
In its delta,
a field opens.

Square miles of grassy pillows-
in circular confines,
bordered by an arbor fence.

I stop to rest my head,
on bramble and branch alike,
beneath a hazy sky-
covered in an opaque canopy.

Nothing enters the frame,
and where stars should be,
clouds loom overhead.

The moon breaks,
piercing the veil,
a firefly flickering in a grayed-out lid.

I find myself enjoying the stillness,
ease giddily into the silence,
like a child swaddled-
stargazing in a cloudy sky.

I shut my eyes,
letting natural music take me…
and just as I get comfortable,
the lid is removed,
the gray dissipates in a cycles trade-
and it begins to rain.

White

In our caverns tight,
during sable night,
a stalactite might
break, dropping of fragments quite-
ghastly and large, but fright
and fear did incite
the blinding sight
produced by neon light-
reflecting bright
off visage right,
to boldly ignite
off an opal meteorite
that this atmosphere did not invite.
But just for the sake of being polite,
we let it shatter our shrouded midnight-
we raised our fists but could not fight...
and that color of death is but a vile white.

Chiasmus

Sidewalks run across themselves
as they run across the sidewalks.
Crosswalks explain themselves, cross…walk…
as they cross over their own nature.
Intersections intersect more intersections
as they intersect those still-
pedestrians inserting themselves in
new, yet entirely uninteresting, introductions.

Horse drawn carriages, drawn poorly.
Swaying gig lamps,
and motor cars whizzing by.
All under the watchful eye of Westminster,
the hands overlapping,
clapping joyously
and still here overlapping-
hands in applause.

Chiasmus-
in its most mediocre form
forming mediocre moments.

Birthmark (:)

I bear a mark on my arm
that comes from nowhere:
but coincidence
and luck if that's what
helps you sleep at night.

Two dots shaped just like this:
placed just below the bow
of my normal, average, boring elbow
that has no meaning beyond it
being there and not being somewhere else.

I didn't get it from anyone.
It's not a torch I carry
or a product of legacy-
I am more in the business
of being a better ancestor
then a descendant anyhow.

Just as the two dots that
line my ordinary skin,
I'll make my own mark,
carry my own torch,
create my own meaning,
and place it wherever the hell I want.

Whirlwind

It should be remembered,
what is said
of he who sows the wind.
He who makes every field a visit-
every town a drive by
And every state a fly-over.
Every place he walked-
well... he was just passing through.

At every party he was a stranger.
he made no friends,
nor took no wife-
for it is a hell of a lot harder
to hit a bullseye
on a moving target.

Any house he'd ever called home
would crumble and break,
rot and erode,
burn and wither-
and blow away just the same.

I've heard them call him
a hundred names,
and I'll probably hear a hundred more:
a vagabond, a rolling stone,
a roamer, a rambling man,
there for a moment
and gone in the next-
as sure as driftwood over rolling tides;
racing down rapids
in the deft hands of white water.

But my favorite name-
is the one the war men gave.
For as he'd reach for the door
and turn the handle,
the gusts would swell
as he picked up his heels-
taking up the sand
and leaving a cloud of dust
in his orphic wake.

It was in the eye of his hurricane
that they dubbed him...

48

He was the one,
that they called the whirlwind.

The Fact That They Fade

Some scars nick your skin
and take a few minutes to scab over-
the kind of cuts
you forget even happened.

Some scars make you bleed a bit.
Drops seep out quietly,
and red stains force you to give pause,
stop what you're doing and grab a bandage.

Some scars go right down to the bone,
leave you reeling, grasping for support
and gasping for air-
the ones that need help to heal.

The universal constant here
is that they do scab and scar-
and it's the fact that they fade
that lets you know you're alive.

Woodchipper

I've got to wonder…
are woodchippers genuinely chipper
about chipping wood chips?
Would a woodchipper even be chipper?
It certainly chips,
but would it?
Would its metal basin
(with which the chipping occurs)
chip away at wood,
and would it be content in its
dispatching of its woody contents.
Would a woodchipper…
be chipper?
I just want to know…

Granite Countertop

A pearlescent streak runs through,
the sporadic peppering of black and white
stars hang high in a beige sky.
Coarse, granular shards array themselves
in almost ethereal formation…
An igneous invasion of a paradoxically organic kind.
That stone has stood stalwart and stationary atop an oaken base,
reflecting the luminous light off of its freshly lacquered surface.
Like an amateur astronomer,
I found myself gazing into endless space…
There, in the comfort of my own kitchen.

Esoteric Universality

What I really mean is buried,
hidden under lock and key.
My intentions masqueraded,
behind the veil of esoteric universality.

Though this desire seems deceptive,
and as troubling as that might be—
my hope is you'll remain receptive...
despite the obscure and veiled decree.

I wish you could relate to it,
maybe find a meaning to hold and own,
though these phrases I struggle to transmit
are tenuous fruits, arduously grown.

For in this dance, there's a kind of grace,
where secrets silently convene...
and a universal, timeless space
emerges from the in-between.

A whispered echo, softly heard,
beyond my own mind's clanging plea,
a truth without a spoken word,
resounding eternally.

So look within, beyond the known,
into the depths where uncertainties roam,
In the words, the essence, (not just my own)
find your truth, and your own way home

BRANCH FOUR:
"LOVE & IDIOSYNCRASIES"

Fish and Cherries

I stood below an awesome power.
Gale forces that cut the air from
silver chariots that detached their spokes
and outstretched their arms toward celestial giants…
I stood below the magnum opus
of the ones who dared to touch the sky.

Through winds and vastness
I met your gaze,
crossing the expanse of open atmosphere.
I wondered how, from so far away,
you could see me so clearly.
You looked afraid,
afraid of damnation- divine judgment.
You feared Zeus's wrath the
way that a child fears the dark,
and when the gray clouds brewed overhead,
and the storm came banging
against your carriage's walls,
your eyes widened, and what was once
Eden's in your mind, sank to grief.

But if you asked me to,
I would plunge my arms in a forge's hearth,
and coat my hands in molten iron…
I'd tip my fingers with lead…
and stand as Apollo did on Olympus's peak
so, the gods may deem me prideful…
scoff at my hubris…
and smite me in her place.
I could be your lightning rod.

If you asked me to
I'd swallow glass and filaments alike,
shred my gums and cut my tongue
chewing against the shards and grain.
I would be your night light,
glowing brightly and bravely,
to turn off and on at your leisure.

We would go together
the way that fish and cherries would:
nonsensical in practicum,

ostrobogulous in theorem,
and wayward in design.
But nonsense is a drafting tool,
design is fickle,
and theory can only take you so far.

A Rather Odd Seating Arrangement

The sun has packed its bags and
departed for eastern advent.
The dog has stopped his barking,
the television fades to black.

They've gone upstairs, the cacophony has ceased,
and you are alone again in the shade.
You sit on the countertop,
a rather odd seating arrangement...
it reflects back to you...
a salt and pepper, peppered, checkered constellation,
from the white light of your computer screen.

You repeat this nightly.
You play Billie Holiday just loud enough
to ring in your eardrums,
but not so loud that the dog will wake,
and bark again as he had done moments ago.

You begin to wonder what curse you bare,
why the solace you found in solitude expired.
You question why when you stare into the abyss...
nothing stares back.

There is no sentience in the shade,
no meaning in the dark.
Shadows do not bare teeth,
but neither do they embrace.

I, dear friend am seated in a vacuum,
I will not soon forget this void,
I will live in it, I was born in it,
I love neither it, nor it loves me,
It simply is, as am I.
And as I am, so are you.

Only, you are seated in a warmer place,
with warmer hues and warmer ground.
Even in the shade, under which you rest,
the light peers through.

As these constants persist,
I pray that one night consists,
of me lying in that shade with you,
letting the light beam through the leaves and stab my eyes.

Or perhaps you'll join me on the granite,
seat yourself just there on the island,
and we'll hit the light switch...
laughing under the violet glow,
about damages done,
the wars we've won,
and all that may fall between the cracks.

I Have This Fear...

I have this fear
that love is just-
a futile, fickle farce.

Must I be damned
to youthful lust?
To vacuous discourse,
in the meager lighting...
of heartless hollow halls.

A baron in station,
yet barren in basis.
Like pitted peaches,
rotting irrevocably
under the harsh indifference
of temporal passage.

I have this fear,
that on festive eve,
with smoke alight and fill'd cup.
The phone would ring,
and I'd pick up...
and those I love,
they would be gone-
lost to cycles,
or heavenly locus.

I have this fear,
the floor will open,
and I'd be swallowed-
condemned to oubliettes,
with mirrors for walls
that reveal to me truths
that I have spent a lifetime
running from.

Forced to see myself...
in unvarnished light;
the whole of me-
in my wretched entirety.

I have this fear,
of stopping by a snow filled wood
as Frost had done,
accompanied by solemnity-
and a little horse in tow.
And rather than shift my boots
step by step over frozen ground,
I instead allow the cold to envelop me,
forsaking the promises I've made
over an innumerable span
of beautiful moments.
trading the good of years,
for the anguish of a second.

I have this fear,
that my life will part no seas...
change no wind, fill no sails,
and touch no heart.
Nor pen anything of substance,
remaining an unlit star...
among a constellation of supernovas.
An inconsequential existence,
a pot not filled,
a life unlived.

I have this fear,
of fear itself.
The gnawing of mangled teeth
snarling at me,
a beast lying in wait,
shrouded by an abyssal cloak.

Its jaws, sharp and serrated,
clutch me without the intent
of relinquishing control-
for panic attacks me,
under the black hole-
of gruesome expectation.

See, I have these fears,
I have them all.
Some sparingly,

some all at once,
and some come and go
like tavern-inn patrons.
They come indiscriminately
in daydreams, in twilight,
or any number of ways and times.
But they arrive, unpack,
make themselves comfortable,
kick up their feet,
and stay awhile.

Diminished

You broke me down to the smallest pieces.
You broke me down to the smallest...
You broke me down to?
You broke me down,
you broke me.
You broke-
you?

Read

Through dry throats and choked words, I…
make the choice, the proclamation of what I'm like,
convince myself that I'm worthy to tell you.

Resigned freedom is not free will.
But you already knew that didn't you?
I'm the first to arrive and the last to go,
and relentlessly trust that truth will out,
though I guess I function better without than with…
struggling to explain myself in the raw entirety of me.

Are these lines trite? Yes.
Read the last words, do they connect? Or…
is it all just one resounding no?

Last

Last,
meaning final
but also, the most recent.
The last time I saw you
will also be the last time
that I see you.

Moments aren't built
to last,
time doesn't construct itself.
It doesn't choose,
and sometimes, neither do we.

Though it's the last thing
that I ever wanted.
you're the last thing
that I need.

Mold

To hold something.
To mold something.
To hold in your hands,
that which you have never held.
To take from nothing,
to reach in-
to grab from places
that you have never dared
reach before.

To love.
To really love.
You must open your arms
and open your heart
to joys
and to sorrows
undreamt of
in your philosophy.

Home

I know it's strange to tell you in a poem.
Words fail me, and thoughts remain as just that.
So long as I draw breath, you'll have a home.

When springs green garments make their presence known,
my hands envelop that skin you tear at.
I know it's strange to tell you in a poem.

When summer's singe kisses skin, and waves all foam,
seek me when crashing torrents brawl and combat.
So long as I draw breath, you'll have a home.

When autumn blows and seasoned leaves all roam,
orange hues never once seemed to fall flat.
I know it's strange to tell you in a poem.

When winter falls and all has lost its chrome,
and our once vivacious colors go matte,
so long as I draw breath, you'll have a home.

Though castles fall and burn like Caesar's Rome,
my unfledged fear has flown and stayed thereat.
I know it's strange to tell you in a poem,
so long as I draw breath, you'll have a home.

Topaz Twilight

A strawberry moon blooms over the shore,
gleaming with blinding sight.
A rosebud plucked from a stratospheric vine,
whose rays dismantled all that was dreary,
and vanquished qualms and fright.

Maybe it was hope's embrace,
that fraudulent usurpers might,
that enthralled, enraptured, entangled me,
in the warmth of a midsummer's night.

Maybe it was amity that grazed me,
or infatuations vicious bite.
Or twisted brambles ensnaring appendages,
fed by fear, and shock, and spite.

Maybe it was the look you gave,
or a trick of orange light,
or the way your fingers peeled from mine,
in the haze of that topaz twilight.

Maybe it was something I said,
for I was surely tricked by light.
See your fingers never met with mine
under the cloak of that topaz twilight.

Yes, your heart had closed, and your head decided,
there was no end to tunneled light,
just an end to me, for that train is coming,
barreling through the fog of that topaz twilight.

The end dear friend, is written here-
under the glow of citrine lamplight.
My contritions plastered with ink and paper,
in the safety of that topaz twilight.

I pray our stars align again,
converging under the constellations light,
my comet lips crash into yours,
under the incandescence of that topaz twilight.

Geography

I am what you could call
an unfledged adventurer.
Happening upon a most mesmerizing landmass;
a gorgeous glen, crystal rivers
running through more rapidly
in this fertile season.
My rugged boots introduced to soil,
dirt soft and supple like skin.
I spearhead through...
nature's boon opened itself up,
and what reveals itself is
the vast and beautiful wood-
that has stood here, long and luscious-
for centuries uncounted.

I find myself enamored.
The sensual sensations of senses stimulated
by varied texture and scenery.
I find myself feeling and fondling foliage and ferns-
my hands run over the rocks,
tiny riptides rippling over-
dew from the runoff is the only remainder.
Eyes that swim across the curves created by the
peaking and valleying of hill laden terrain.

If you have ever reached the highest crest,
where the view is not done justice
by the word "spectacular-"
you must know that the real spectacle
is the avalanche.
Snowballing in a slow build-
giving way to tremors...
the aftershocks of little earthquakes.

My dearest earth,
my solid world,
the descents from your rise and fall
are to my ears a hummingbird's call-
sweet and vibrant,
flitting and fleeting.
But, be this moment fickle,
regular, daily, or a mere moment passed...
I have loved traversing your geography.

Art

If the breaking of a heart
were a finer form of art
then you'd be Van Gogh-
and I'd be *Starry Night*.

I caught your later works
and peeked behind the curtain
of a canvas you are painting
In the present tense.
Your work in progress
formed with perfect brushstrokes-
and masterful shading.

Your display grew from the bedroom
to the finest museums,
the hanging of *Sunflowers and Irises*,
the scenic views of
The Bedroom in Arles' and
A Cafe Terrace at Night-

But none, dear painter,
could ever truly compare
to that first creation of yours-
your magnum opus...
your bonafide hit...
your real, true, genuine masterpiece.

Cigars in the Rain

A dead man's kiss-
a bed of embers,
withering and warring
all at once.

Your paradoxical dance,
your scorching mouth,
my burning throat-
my singed fingertips.

The casing peels,
the scent dissipates-
the flame collapses inward
on itself-

fire pushes outward
against the wind
and under droplets sent
from beyond our leveled view.

Like cigars in the rain,
all vigor has left,
and all that burns is waste
to be scattered along the dirt.

That last utterance
of your accursed name-
lingers on my lips
with notes of coffee and tobacco.
Still, I drive through the storm,
my arm hanging out the driver side window-
of my brand new car.
Raise it to my lips-
and take one....
last...
slow...
drag.

Fault Lines

There, in my unworthy palms…
nestled between the crags and valleys,
and the lines and calluses…
I held gently on to what I now believe
to be the greatest thing they have ever had
the distinct honor of holding.

Day broke over an umbral horizon.
white hot light came pouring over the crust…
it was an igneous formation.
That light cooled, hardened, and fell softly…
into the cache with which I found you in.

You, dear gem…
held in your interior…
a kaleidoscopic display of wonder,
and it left all who dared stare
in a state of mesmer.
Your light, like Gyges to his flock,
led my eyes to your crystalline figure…

I lifted your form from the brutal ground,
though you seemed content to stay.
I placed you on satin pillows,
with velvet skin and golden tassels
that could not match your perfection…
But I yearned to keep up.
All that surrounded you,
lost its luster under your light.

I spoke to you in a whisper,
for fear that too loud a vibration
would send shockwaves through your grain…
I recited the words and works
that I had waited a lifetime to share.
You took it in…
and you glowed with a radiance,
that dared the dawn to burn brighter.

Cruel indifference prevails; it always does.
I approached your temple and lifted you-
as I had done before.
And, from my hands you fell,
swiftly, suddenly, and without reproach.
You landed at just the right angle…

the grain split, the cracks fissured,
the fault lines ran through, and eruption was imminent.

All that was once warm and bright...
turned hot and blinding.
I picked up your pieces,
and my hands were seared.
I grasped again, desperately, but each time
I was met with that familiar sting.
I knew that the charring of my flesh meant only one thing.
You hated me, and you always would.
And so, I left you there, scattered and shattered.
You left me with no other option.

To this day-
be it in dreams, or memory alone,
or a sepulcher by the sea...
I still caress you in my palms,
and speak to you in a tone so hush'd
that not even the wind could hear.
If your hatred were to burn eternal,
and scorched earth be your choice...
know that I harbor no greater contrition,
than the day the fault lines split.

Desireless Fire

I wanted to boldly burnish your soul's sword
and leave a polished luster,
but you always found my lack of lust
a little less than lackluster.
I never wanted steam,
an impermanent extemporized dream,
because feelings fade and castles fall-
foundations of sand aren't as solid as they seem.
To be to brave, to be true, to scorch away the liars,
to watch the embers fly from the coals of a desireless fire.

The senseless sleep of bodies unconnected,
heads turned over, arms folded neatly,
a cold embrace of the solo form.
I wish for no such innate inanity, nothing crude,
wishes that never aligned with sleeping with-
but rather, next to.
With heads facing towards,
arms wrapped tightly,
a warm embrace of the coupled form...
to warm you in the pyres of my desireless fire.

Parcel

If there was just one parcel...
of knowledge I'd impart...
It'd be to lead with your head-
yet still satiate your heart.

For those who feel-
with leagues ungauged...
run the horrid risk-
of living caged-

in murky depths,
in loveless tides,
through gasping breaths,
through stifled strides.

To you, dear flame-
do not spare a thought-
to wretched game,
nor battles fought.

Focus now on comfort,
live in warless peace,
know that your needs come first,
in this new year's lease.

May this passage find you,
may you read it well,
may its message ring true,
may its secrets tell:
a million truths you can't convey...
a thousand breaks you cannot heal...
a hundred aches you can't display...
a single sentiment you'll always feel...

Strange

How strange I that must look,
how uncouth that I must seem…
it's high time that I filled a book,
with runoff from my fountain's dream.

How strange I am in actuality,
how baffling I must appear…
for conversing still with frightened glee
with the specters conjured from dread and fear.

How strange you must perceive me,
how right you really are…
for the roots of this demented tree,
run deep and long and far.

How strange it is to walk unfettered,
how rare it is to speak unchained.
Blind incoherence to those unlettered,
is 'Der Flowhalzer' to critics trained.

How strange is a series without the fillers?
How incongruous the story presents…
when innocents are the silent killers,
and salvation is only for he who repents.

How strange, how crude, how out of line…
how eerie it is when disaster strikes.
Elation retires in this heart of mine,
too beaten and weary to chase your lookalikes.

Auburn Eyes

I loved you.
I mean, I almost did.
Or- I might have.
Or maybe I never did.
Maybe I never loved you at all.

I saw you.
I mean, I thought I did.
I really tried,
or maybe I didn't try hard enough.
Maybe I never really saw you at all.

I thought that you,
you and only you
could see me-
I mean really see me.

But now I know
that only lies were
surmised behind those
auburn eyes.

Maybe we both
never really saw each other
at all.

Could Be

There has been no kiss,
no embrace, nor fleeting moments grace-
that compares to ones that
you're a part of love...

for even in the sable secrecy
of a room caressed by shade-
in darkest dream,
where all might lay
mute and dreadful...
I am lifted by your involuntary glow
spilling out from you-
for you could not help
if that light of yours
all but outshone day.

Though this heart of mine-
is long since benighted-
and my flame is but merely a flicker...
It has long since been decided-
I shan't rebuff, refute, or bicker.
See, this heart is yours
though it beats in me,
it has served its tours,
battered as could be.

Do not leave me stoned,
in this barren hall,
where the floorboards grown,
and the pillars fall.
Do not leave me trapped
in my own eternal feud,
of gainless loss,
and ideas crude.

Stay with me now,
learn what could be in store-
could be that we're doomed to a cycle?
Or is it possible...
that we could be more?

Argonaut

I met you in the
most jam-packed place possible-
where the music was loud
and the noise of the crowd
drowned out every word
we'd dare exchange.

I remember how the halls
panned out, each floor
a circle of hell in its own right,
and how you, every morning,
would run into the serpent's mouth
unwillingly, yet gallantly.

I found you in the darkest corner-
hands tucked, knees folded,
as your arms coiled 'round.
I descended the stairs,
heard your shoes crash against them
Behind me
        one
           step
              at
                a
                  time
Until I turned,
and the doors were swung open-
at the base of a
crimson painted staircase;
you were gone.

But you know-
I would've walked through hell
to bring you out
of the underworld that you created
in your own mind.

The Girl Who Loves Everyone

I'd been apathetic for years-
the chronic kind of numb,
but over skipping stones and sarcastic tones...
my life had finally begun.
It was an abstruse affair,
one rooted not in salacious fun,
but I've known no greater joy since I met
the girl who loves everyone.

She'll don an emerald dress,
take the floor, have her fun.
When the night has run too long
and the hours have all but gone,
her last dance's twirl was spun,
and everyone has found their one-
I'll peel myself off the wall for
the girl who loves everyone.

I had always been told that this
drab day would come;
it was a mere stipulation,
a simple setting of the sun.
The last magic's been exhausted,
her patience was all but done-
despite the ever-present truth- she's
the girl who loves everyone.

I've been told by the many that
I should pack my bags and run,
but no man with fierce conviction
can truly change his center sum.
It's a course I cannot alter;
you don't reverse bullets from a gun.
Figures, I just had to be the one-cursed to love
the girl who loves everyone.

In The Dead of Winter

As Frost performs its covert ministry,
and window panes
and windshields alike
glaze over with thin
sheet-like layers
of wayward ice-
I'll stare out
into that barren terrain...
admiring the juxtaposition
of the cold outside...
and the warmth within.

You hear the regale'd tales-
jubilant glee under
the summer's heat,
waves in – waves out.
The sun glares
over ivory skin
that trickles with falling dew.
Transparent paint
on human canvases.

You'll hear of fall's new leaves,
falling fast and hard
from the branches of tentative trees,
reluctantly relinquishing that which it:
spawned, formed, grew, created.

And every April,
those same green garments
of subtle spring soar
under wanton skies-
the flying kite,
the returning flock,
the movement in the water-
the rippling a harbinger
of successful hibernation.

But me, in my (perhaps needless)
separation conspire – and still here admire –
that winter's eve fire
within the confines of
my bedroom, the flickering reflecting
off the window panes before me.
Just as the day

that I first saw light-
when sapphire eyes
met paneled ceilings
and fluorescent lights...

I fell in love
in the dead of winter.

BRANCH FIVE:
"BORN FORTY"

Atlas

A man,
who was loved by few
in his youth-
once told me that
he and I were the same.

This man, with worn hands-
hands whose lines and scars
form a collage
of all of his yesterdays.
He who took a rock
and turned it into a rocket ship.

He sees himself in me-
he sees the world we've overcome-
or are trying to,
and told me I'm not alone.
But in one regard,
he was wrong.

See, before my lungs
ever once inhaled
the sweet poison
we call our atmosphere-
I was expected to be great.
The kind of great that surpassed
the storybooks
and history books
and all expectations created
in fables or in fairytales.

But this man,
who knew not of the subject-
as it was beyond
his vast (yet limited) experience-
did not know that he was
weightless, and therefore-
expectation did not mire
the very origin
of his achievement.
But for me,
and for those
who have been sentenced
to carry the weight of another's world

and their burdens in our hearts
do not wish it upon another.
For you see,
I shoulder that burden
and I call it an honor-
but that doesn't make it
any less heavy.

You do not want my world-
and the worlds I hold-
you do not want
my life-
you are no Atlas.

Revenant

Every time you rise,
you return from the spectral plane-
your bed and ghoulish sheets
are an amateur Lazarus pit.

You watch people in their
various minutia, doomed
to witness the occasional Memento Mori-
in their eyes
at sudden loss or
poor blood pressure.

But these are lost on you.
You are but a revenant-
you walk this earth
with the scars and cynicism
to prove that you have died
a thousand small deaths.

So, watch- you soulless phantasm
from beyond the windows
and envy their fear of death-
for they are neither wights nor wraiths,
nor a phantom visitant.

They cling to life in a manner
you wish that you could-
they cling and claw,
a handless shadow in the mirror
could never possibly understand.

Thunder & Lightning

Sometimes I goad the lightning-
simply because I can.
I kick and scream and curse and spit…
to feel more like a "man."

Sometimes I yell at thunder
to see if I can be just as loud-
a booming roar that splits the sky
and nestles in a cloud.

Sometimes I ride the lightning
that surges through my veins-
and let the wild hands of impulse
take hold of the reins.

Sometimes I roll with the thunder
that is beating in my chest;
each boom a cry, all sound no fury-
hard pressed to find genuine rest.

Sometimes my head is all thunder & lightning,
just storms to brew and hell to raise.
But when I asked the doctor "why?"
she said, "it's just a phase."

Everything, All at Once

There's a music of our own design,
a despondent harmony unearthed
by how we long and pine.
So we cast a new spell, a seemingly impenetrable shell-
is it tangible? Fictitious?
There's no way to tell.

Because there's cracks in that armor,
a fortress unsecured.
My head is a harbor
for the hardships I've endured.
Docks for the meager,
ports for the bleak,
perpetually vying for an impossible peak.

It doesn't matter where you seek,
be it by wooded creek or
the cities' blinding streak.
You can run for years,
you could hide for months-
when you face up to nothing...
 you deal with everything all at once.

It's the truth of the trade,
a fact of the craft,
bury your head in the sand
or in your own daily graft,
there is no circumvention,
no semantics nor nuance...
when you face up to nothing,
you deal with everything all at once.

Rubber Boy

Here he comes!
The rubber boy!
        Bouncing!
           Down!
              the
                hill!
And there he glides
with his Switzerland stride…
            dying
                on
                  no
                    hill!
The malleable man!
The plastic man!
Ambivalent and wishy-washy
           as
             any
               one
                could
                  be!

The Space Between Ink Blots

I'm convinced that
my brain is the equivalent
of a psychopath writing a love letter.
He holds his pen
as if it were a knife,
sheathed in the squishy holster
of my bleeding head.

I suppose this
brand of morbidity
is undesirable-
but to this I say:
"Get used to it."

This mind of mine,
(like all minds in their genesis)
was blank paper,
a tabula rasa,
till the knife came through
and red ink flooded the page.

In my later years I have stepped back,
let it settle,
let the "ink" dry-
taken a long hard look at it.
It's less of a flood than I thought
and more of a series
of unsightly blotches
taking up all the good rooms-
unwanted tenants...
squatters in my weary headspace.

But the lesson here
is that there is still room to write,
to sneak stories
in the space between ink blots.

To make worlds within the words,
poems in a paper multiverse-
each giving you a chance
to do it the right way.

This action,
this writing-
it's a revenge of sorts,
but more than this-
it's a reclamation,
or perhaps a declaration.
Perhaps we aren't merely
the sum total of our stories.

Damage

Damage begets damage.
Damaged men
damage women.
Damaged women
damage sons.
Damaged sons become
damaged men.
Damage begets damage-
or so the story goes.

Old Fashioned
-Featured on "Calliope: A Poetry Podcast"

Twenty-one revolutions.
Twenty-one bottles.
A salute to each year-
this is not my style.
I'd much prefer to spend it familiarly-
famillially-
family.

Crystalline glass, rounded,
molded, mounted in merry palms.
Studded exteriors, running calloused fingers along them-
I always preferred the feel
over the look.
Glass.

Rocks line its bottom,
frozen lake stones,
a sharded gravel coast,
sinking deep-
icy transiens.
Ice.

Meetings, conversations,
maraschino mind-melding,
luxuriation in luxardo syrup.
Sweet and bold,
bold and sweet,
sweetly bold-
cherries.

They're all here now.
This culmination, this table-
lined with the fruits of your labor.
The runoff of your toils,
the twisting of a sharpened peel-
torch it, let the aroma waft-
burned citrus peels.

Sours shade these evenings too-
sordid and salacious on your tongues.
This is what regret would taste like
if you could bottle it.
Arguments, empty chairs, stained tablecloths,
orange bitters.

But the sweetness of the chew,
the activation of salivary glands
on granular joy. The gray area.
To be both good and bad,
right and righteous-
when you're older,
it's all muddled.
Turbinado sugar.

So pop out from the oak-
be not a stow-away, barrel aged.
Have intentions of making a mark.
I'd prefer mine be left on a paper trail,
much less than a digital footprint.
Cap it off with a red wax seal-
bourbon.

Young man, enter the room.
You cannot breathe the smoke...
of mundane merriment-
you're the man out of time,
the relic of a bygone age,
and that might all be true, but...
it's possible that I could just be-
Old Fashioned.

To All the Memories I'll Never Make

They say you depart the kingdom of childhood
when you realize your own mortality.
Velvet knapsacks corralling
cruel patches of wretched memory,
slung over our backs, seemingly
never to be relinquished.

Adolescents make for hapless vagabonds,
forced to embark on a blameless campaign-
where the ghosts of my past haunt my present
because they will never be in my future.

It is the mark of a maddened mind,
to still long for things unknown,
but before dusk departs for the break of day,
there's a few farewells I'd ought to say.

To all the memories I'll never make...
to all the chances I'll never take,
to all the hope I'll never hold,
to all the things that don't stay gold,
to all the cards I'll never play,
to all the words I'll never say,
to all the fires I'll never light
to all the rounds I'll never fight-

May you paint tuskless elephants
and sunsets in a storybook studio,
may you spin in the beautiful galas held in my memory palace.
I'd have loved you long and well
in a different moment...
but the march king plays his song
and time walks in tune,

And I along with it...
And I along with it.

The Hard Part of the Night

The fear that I fight is neither spiders nor flight,
but a fear of fear itself.
To want, to need, to hope, to dream…
to wake up during the hard part of the night.

Those hours ooze fabricated fright.
Simple objects like windows, or an antique bookshelf.
Nothing is ever as innocent as it may seem…
when you wake up during the hard part of the night.

The tossing, the turning, the hatred of the light.
The obligatory mirror check- "you're not so bad yourself."
Be warned, your hands may splinter
on the jagged wooden beam…
The pains of waking up
during the hard part of the night.

Valor doesn't matter, neither
strength nor guts nor might,
when you face the dark
accompanied only by oneself.
Stay quiet, dead quiet,
never let them hear you scream…
when you find yourself alone
during the hard part of the night.

You'll always find yourself alone
during the hard part of the night.

Modern Day Siegfried (Dragons)

Some days,
you either slay the dragon
or chase it-
some days you'd do both.

Most days,
I just don't have it in me-
and I let myself be swallowed.
A modern-day Siegfried
I am not…

The Jumping Boy

The jumping boy jumped in the sand,
and let the grains slip through his hand-
he played and took his share of wonder
with his friends, his boys, his merry band.
The jumping boy jumped in the sand.

The jumping boy jumped into bed,
he let her hands run over his head.
He loved in a way he couldn't grasp-
till the words ran out and all was said.
The jumping boy jumped into bed.

The jumping boy jumped off to war,
with earnest hope he could be more
but that chip lay heavy on his shoulder,
so he traded himself to settle a score.
The jumping boy jumped off to war.

The jumping boy jumped down a bottle,
be it oxy or Vicodin, or whiskey or vodka.
Life in the fast lane blurs lines and lights alike,
the transmission cranked, the engine full throttle.
The jumping boy jumped down a bottle.

The jumping boy jumped towards the edge.
Forsaken bonds and a meaningless pledge,
wrapped around his ears and inside his mind-
his horses ran, no more bets to hedge.
The jumping boy jumped from the ledge.

Superhero

Comic Panel 1-

A little boy
sits buckled in a chair,
twirling his curly hair.
Just like you did when
you were his age-
though his is lighter and longer.

You watch him twirl and wither
because mommy and daddy
haven't put solid food
in his body for all six
of his liquid years.

You can't save him.
Call CPS all you want,
you can't save him.

Comic Panel 2-

A young man-
younger in his desires
then he is in station-
his face likens yours.

You can come a long way
and in some regards,
still go nowhere.
Push him along,
help him,
move that which he says
is immovable-
love that which was deemed unlovable.
Try- try to fix him,
tell him they were wrong
about a ghost running his machine...

You can't save him.
He doesn't want to be saved.
You can't save him.

Comic Panel 3-

A strong man,
a quiet one too,
just as strong as is he is quiet,
just like you wish you could be-

look him in the eye,
watch as his meet the floor...
tell him he didn't fail,
tell him he did good...
tell him his best was enough,
and tell him it all meant something.

Save him from his own
warped definitions of success and failure,
mend his soles, the holes
where his toes poke through-
mend his soul, the pieces
he broke off and placed in you.
But you are asleep while
he works the graveyard shift...

You can't save him.
You don't have the years
or the courage to speak.
You can't save him.

Comic Panel 4-

An old woman,
older in her mind
then she is in her body
just like yours.

You watch as her skin
heals over (not completely).
It can't, it never will,
from the wounds the world inflicted.

You can't save her-
break down all the doors you want.
You can't save her.

Comic Panel 5-

You notice slight after slight,
injury after injury,
death after life-
you see it in faces
behind tired eyes.

In ragged clothes atop ragged skin,
on Salvation Army suits,
and birthday suits,
and superhero suits,
and whatever kind of suits suit
a good enough facade.

Serve as armor,
serve as triage,
serve as gauze that cover up
gunshot wounds-
band aids, no aid, AIDS epidemics,
death parades, body bags,

peel your eyes open,
you're a hero, right?
You are blessed to see it all,
Now go save them!
Go save them; it's your job!

You are cursed to see it all-
Now go save them...
"I can't."

Pragmatic

Some days you
practically lived in a library-
though those days did
not come as often
as you feel
they should have.

You pin quotes
against a wooden board
hanging loosely off
the dry-wall-
pinning the artist
against the pragmatist
and halfheartedly chase
your only dream.

So to you I ask
(as both a "practical person"
and dreamer too)
would it really be
"pragmatic" to be alive
and do anything less
than what you really want to do?

Mud

Sometimes you're in the shit-
or you're treading water-
or you're wading in the mud.

But when you're in
any of those lovely substances
for a moment too long

one starts to look like the other,
and you sure as shit should not drink shit-
just because you're thirsty.

Prevaricate

Dear writer...
You sit surrounded by an unsightly pile,
a plethora of projects
half done, half not,
all half-never-finished-
and instead of getting to the pith of things...
you take the scenic route in discourse
like a distracted child
chasing a butterfly into
a sharp and nettled rosebush.

You prevaricate more often
then a politician being asked
A "yes" or "no" question.
And frankly-
I hate it.

                    Signed yours truly,
                              - A pissed off reader.

Age and Treachery

I should be writing as a young man should-
drunk off of my own hubris,
choking on my own arrogance-
crowning myself king,
cashing in on the brashness
of my supposed brash nature
bashing my hands against all walls
watching them fall and smiling
at my own godlike strength.
But you will not allow me to
not because of some
benevolent hand of intervention,
but rather because
you are so easily read,
and your tale reads to me
as cautionary.
I watch you drink piss
that you call gold
as you blind yourself
with inebriation, and still,
you remain blind to
the very existence
of your own blind spot.
Your ideas are fossils.
Your words are husks.
Your dreams are tombs.
Your hopes are sepulchers.
And, your thought patterns-
yes the very pith of you
is ancient-
preserving a corpse
encased in amber.
Age and experience
are not a contrast to
youth and exuberance.
When age and treachery
are the true tandem in question-
for experience has jaded you,
nightmare shrouds have shaded you
and every day you're pushing through
the bullshit you say you left behind you.

Ruby Rivers

Sanguine streams trickle tepidly from you,
beige river beds covered by crimson creeks.
Ruby red rivers run rapidly through.

Screams behind gates obstruct the morbid view,
piercing ears and hearts with violent shrieks as
sanguine streams trickle tepidly from you.

No arms were present, but you'd still make due,
for years you've honed your medieval techniques...
Ruby red rivers run rapidly through.

Reflective fragments sever old skin from new,
dead pieces split off as necrosis reeks.
Sanguine streams trickle tepidly from you.

The pooling ceased and left a faded hue.
I watched you pray as the floorboards sprung leaks.
Ruby red rivers run rapidly through.

Crimson tolls paid for deaths cruel avenue-
ferrying souls since the conception of weeks.
Sanguine streams trickle tepidly from you.
Ruby red rivers run rapidly through.

Old Soul

When I was a child,
still marveling at the world's wonder,
I walked in a state of half-mesmer.
Enthralled under youth's enchantment,
I would descend the creaking staircase,
hanging on for dear life to a looping rail;
stepping downward on carpeted plank
in superman socks and opal pajamas,
draped over me like a roman toga.

I remember the man who coined the phrase,
who dubbed me with the moniker...
the man who crowned me king
of a castle I had no intention of ruling.
At first he was a bystander,
a witness to infant joy
through the gaze of cerulean mirrors,
filling his eyes and mine with older joys, tapes of a bygone age-
painting, woodworking, and monster trucks.

"You forget you're talking to a child," he says,
"You were born forty" she says,
"We thought you were thirty" they said,
giggling at the absurdity of thought.
But, absurdity gave way to plausibility.
In a matter of mere moments
spanned throughout the hourglass-
of trying, testing, beautiful, gorgeous years.

If I were given a dime
for each and every time
that those phrases were shoved down my throat-
I would choke on the riches,
spit it out,
and convert to cash my endless change,
my overflowing boon-
and buy myself a good night's sleep.

For sleep scarcely comes
in a mind that was not gifted
with the bliss of forgetting.
I remember the rage mostly...
the rage that built and bubbled, boiling over-reliance.
Rage in too great of an abundance like
crushing weight, rising red tides
crashing against my skull and shoulders-
without reprieve, always present...
you asked me for too much,
you all did,
and you did it every day.

I remember when the dam broke...
how demolition over took the delta-
and washed out the banks.
How nothing that ever was
would ever be as it had been before the flood.
How the hurricanes blew...
and a ghost town remained
in the heart and mind of me.

I remember the moment that childhood ended
before it ever began.
I remember the moment it was cemented,
laid six feet beneath our shined shoes-
a cobble headstone with deep engravings.
It was a rather short distance of years
Between the infinite space of the hyphen.

Even though that spell is broken,
and the eulogies have ended,
the rental on the hearse expired
and the suits returned to the tailors-
I suppose there would be no danger
in letting myself let hope in.
Hope that flipping an aphorism
is not a potential vexation,
and that wisdom is not wasted
on the young.

"You're an old soul, kid."
I know...
I'm alright with it.

BRANCH SIX:
"PLEDGES & OUBLIETTES"

Easy

The fool, his fickle wind ever breezy,
his sound drowned by raging seas - it's uncouth.
Gruesome mouths that dare say "take it easy!"
Knowing not, the ever pertinent truth-
tempered metal is made in cruel forges,
from daily toils and varied trouble.
See, fair fellows lose what makes them gorgeous
after strolls over coals and jagged rubble.
It's the clashing of shining hone'd swords,
that sharpen and whet new etched edges.
The struggle of a dry throat forming words,
that places more meaning in our pledges.
True, the good die young, and the great die younger,
but easy lives do not make men stronger!

The Arbitrary Nature of Arbitrary Ideas

Saussure's idea of the arbitrary
would dictate that the very
language this (and that) sentence
was written in-
does not come from a place
of inherent meaning.

So what is it to say of the "sun" then?
Does it not matter that it will die?
Or will mankind manufacturer
a new one when ours runs out?
Shades of Edison and his stolen lightbulb...

I wouldn't mind it
if some things didn't matter:
power is bullshit, (and relative)
money is useless depending on geolocation,
"society" doesn't exist as a term
depending on who you're talking to.

Strong (yet weak) constructivism...
a barrier of sorts-
between the world and myself.
Between vision and blindness.
Between looking and seeing.
Between hearing and listening.
Between observation and understanding.

Or perhaps
that too,
is an arbitrary idea-
that is arbitrary in nature.

Gray

Sing in the rain,
lay claim to outrageous fortune and immortalized fame,
dance away one hundred nights,
sell a variety of works,
tell them your name.

Shoulder the world at large,
move a mountain in a mere day...
before your body grows old,
your hands turn cold,
and your hair goes gray.

Articulation is a
fickle form of art...
one that wages a war
between the head and the heart.
I feel those neural strings and
cardiac threads begin to fray...
as my body grows old,
my skin turns cold,
and my hair goes gray.

It's arbitrary for you,
with eyes eternally bright,
your blaze interminably alight,
in pearlescent day or onyx night.
You'll still envelop rooms in
brazen blankets that keep the frost at bay-
even after your body grows old,
your skin turns cold,
and your hair goes gray.

My youth's speciously infinite spring
has been all but simply supped,
and dormant volcanic furnaces
can no longer boldly erupt.
So, I may lower my guards and be granted rest
in the truly righteous way...
now that my body's grown old,
my skin has turned cold,
and my hair has gone gray.

The Library I'd Fill

The library I'd fill would span acres and still-
burst o'er the ramparts and scatter beyond the hill.
Its contents would harbor neither drivel nor swill,
flooding towns and countries, not a mere trickle nor spill.
Never, not I, in the library I'd fill.

After an indefinite sequestering and a great deal of motion...
it was the result of loving labor and a sea of great devotion-
the rows became a forest and the paths had spanned an ocean.
I felt drunk on its substance, like a sweet supple potion,
with arrogance abound from a simply pompous notion.

After thumbing through pages and wasting precious hours,
I strayed from the rows and stumbled past the towers-
there was a whisper of sorts, a spark of nebulous powers.
It was a nefarious creature, full of bitters and sordid sours,
he scoured and laid waste with his sunset orange flowers.

The Library I filled span'd acres and still-
burned high o'er the ramparts as ashes scattered beyond the hill.
Its contents never'd harbored neither drivel nor swill,
but it leaked nonetheless in a sad sputtering spill-
impotently watching auburn embers erode the library I'd filled...

Freedom (Imprisonment)

Rows and halls,
seats and chairs,
plastic and wood.
These are cruxes that hold up
both educational institutions
and sanitariums alike.

Young men in libraries-
reading works and ideas
penned by the minds of more
young men in libraries.

We are free thinkers,
supposedly freely thinking-
yet if that were a stipulation-
why are we imprisoned
by the ideas penned by
old men (once young)
slaving away in libraries-
servile as ever to texts and literature
penned by the minds of men
older still than them?

In the context of our lives,
in this modern day-
some works are mere scribblings,
scratched and etched onto concrete walls...
man would do most anything...
to keep their minds occupied.
For even now
should these words be read
days or weeks or years from now...
they'd no longer be considered contemporary
nor relevant to our definition
of modernity.
And would be memorialized
as one of those mere scribblings.

I want us to be free-
free enough to define what freedom is.
The kind of free that caged birds
nor kindred souls could
make known to their hearts,
but deserved to more than
those men mentioned.

Freedom and imprisonment
are not mutually exclusive terms.
We are trapped in our freedom-
and liberated in our cages.
Chained and shackled by concepts,
ironclad in our ways of being-
but running amuck
in the racket of our minds,
and wandering off this beaten path-
is the only way you learn…
that it's all an illusion.

Write

I write to right the ship I wrecked,
to chart a course for syllabic seas,
and after soaking in uncharted waters-
chase the illusive haze of a depth gauge phrase.

I write to right the wrongs you left,
to ask whether it is better to weather weary weathers
that tears tears and ignites your fears-
fears that bore fangs, that moved with deft hands.

To deal in the conceptual.
To question the qualitative qualities
that quantify our being.
Whether that be done in concise or loquacious fashion,
it is done in service of those...
that occupy a space in a heart ever heavy.

Metaphors

One day, maybe someday soon,
you'll wake up and run the numbers.
The amount of time you spent thumbing through a dictionary.
The amount of times you looked up "rhymes with (x)"
The amount of adjectives you threw...
into an already convoluted stanza.

One day, maybe someday soon,
you'll shut the fuck up and accept it:
the fact that nobody knows what you're talking about,
the fact that they scoff at your structure-
the fact that nobody gives a shit...
if your poem was written in dactylic hexameter.

One day, maybe someday soon,
you'll give up the act.
The act of indifference to their gaze,
the act of showmanship you don't possess,
the act in a play that nobody has come to see...
on its opening night.

One day, maybe someday soon,
you'll quit selling the lie,
the lie that the words you peddle are "deep" and "meaningful,"
the lie that your work is "universally esoteric,"
you'll stop trying to embed some stupid hidden message,
in every incessant thing you write.

One day, maybe right now
you'll go free verse on a piece that once had structure.
And say what you actually want to,
rather than what you think sounds good.
Instead of abusing your readers eyes,
and making them suffer through your rambling,
give them something to chew on...
and remember you by.

You don't need to write sonnets, Shakespeare did it better.
You don't need to write villanelles, Dylan Thomas did it better.
The same could be said about an ode and Schiller.
So before you define sanity or end up concussed...
quit banging your head against that particular wall.

Say what it is that you actually feel,
no bells, no whistles, no pageantry.

No rhyme scheme, no meter.
Stop making outlandish comparisons…
like the "tragedy" of putting on shoes that don't fit,
with a notion that you have no place in this world.

Be real, be original,
be honest, be authentic.
Don't be ridiculous, don't be trite,
don't fall into old patterns, don't stagnate.
Stop describing every fucking sunset,
stop counting on your fingers in public…
the amount of syllables for iambic pentameter.
And for God's sake…
enough with the shitty metaphors.

Fire

I wonder where wonder went.
I wonder why I stare out into open air,
open atmosphere spanned out across a burning horizon
painting the sky that autumn orange.
I wonder why I tear at curled hair,
like just because it's thick it won't rip.
I wonder why the air smells like fire.

Fireworks, they boom and streak
across a fog hung sky, stagnating-
umbral and sleek...
but that fire works, performing, burning
all things that dare remain drab and bleak.
That smoke hitchhiking across gale passages,
like packages with express shipping...
watering and stinging my eyes,
staining my shirt (and yours) with forced tears
because the air still smells like fire.

Can't you see that this blaze grows higher?
Each passing glance from the nine to fivers-
the minutia trance, blind men leading those yet blinder-
glazed eyes from either that fog or ignorance,
but I can't seem to ever
tell the difference...
and the air still smells like fire!

We watch indifferently, a planet burning...
artificial forces, brewing, churning-
but those bus wheels just continue turning
as indoctrination is labeled "learning."
We leave our neighbors cold and yearning-
despite the fact-
that the air still smells like fire.

Dry Throat

I can't tell if it's dehydration,
crippling unoriginality,
or just a plain lack of trying...
but no words escape these lips of mine.
Each phrase a convict...
serving a life sentence
in the Alcatraz of my mouth.

I sometimes find that thoughts
are best depraved of daylight...
and metrics given to them in language-
length, width, and height
should be reserved for the kind
of discourse that carries real water.
Perhaps none actually does.

I keep these moments
in mental lockboxes
guarded by pit traps and oubliettes
for I am so fearful
of what those manifestations
could come to mean

These words are a dish
best served never.
And when you ask me
for the product of those
unrealized pledges,
I will tell you that my throat is dry...
and I am shit at multiplication.

Perpetuation

What you would call plagiarism-
I merely dub "perpetuation."
It is in the very nature
of the media cannon
to reflect and refract itself
across time and pages-
from this very paper,
to the stone tablets the
neanderthals would carve vague
looking figures onto
inside of Plato's cave.

Did you really think
that Harry Potter was original?
Watch Star Wars-
and if you thought that was inspired…
read Joseph Campbell.
He too, like all good authors
stole- and got away with it.

See, poetry begets poetry
and art begets art-
music and melody,
rhythm and whatever else
you wish to compare.

Nothing is original-
not even Werther's...
Get used to it.

Modernity

I wasn't aware
that the price of "innovation"
would be that
when I sit down to dinner-
the phones would eat first.

I didn't know that apps
would be applications
for partners to spend
one turn of an existence with-
to take an image
and convert it from a PNG
to a marriage license.

I had no clue that schools
would begin to liken Orwell novels-
we tell them what to work on
and when to work on it.
We post guards in stairways,
and hallways, outside restrooms too.
Make them give their John Hancock
to take a piss.

I'm beginning to wonder
why education looks more like religion-
a mass indoctrination,
a means of subjugation
to perpetuate mass repression…

I wish for a change
in our modern expression-
I crave a real fucking renaissance-
I want to see a paper
of ninety-five solutions
nailed to school district buildings…

and as much as I
would hate to break
from "compliance"
or "conformity…"
I would be rather remiss
if I did not raise concerns
about the status of "modernity."

Gold

I'll spend my years in search of gold,

an interminable trial of how much these hands can hold.
It's true that fortune favors the bold,
so I will not rest 'till the final nuggets sold,
on a resplendent lifetime spent chasing gold.

In a Yukon hearth I got my start,
as an apprentice to one with a miner's heart,
bore the brunt of the hard labor, swung the ax, pulled the cart.
In the deepest cavern, never placed upon the chart,
stood the grandest pure ore, an ethereal piece of art.

Neither man nor woman could stop their staring,
I'd stand before kings and dine with the barons,
ignored fallacies in kind and snubbed every red herring.
But the galas all ended, the lights no longer glaring,
there's a sensation, a weight, one I'd been oblivious to bearing.

See I'd spent my years in search of gold,
but never found someone these hands could ever hold.
Bold as I may be, fortune no longer favors the old,
and my last pernicious nugget has finally sold,
the final nugget of a lifetime wasted on chasing gold.

Dust

Can you recall the moment that you broke?
The boulder met your shoulder, ruination.
Just a pile of dust, and a cloud of smoke.

Young Sisyphus knew not the hubris that he spoke,
he hoisted that stone and damned damnation.
Can you recall the moment that you broke?

Pillars crumbled round Sampson's golden cloak,
earnest weakness born of sweet temptation.
Just a pile of dust, and a cloud of smoke.

Dante's ferry among circles did evoke,
desire for a divine cremation.
Can you recall the moment that you broke?

When Pompeii burst and toppled common folk,
that rubble harbored no lamentations,
just a pile of dust, and a cloud of smoke.

A thousand absolutes, now? A mere joke,
the ignorant cheer with joyous ovation.
Can you recall the moment that you broke?
Just a pile of dust, and a cloud of smoke.

Compiler

You sit aimlessly, sodden-
dowsed and awash in the blue light
from your glorified typewriter.
You reference quills and ink,
as if they were filial companions-
brothers in arms.

But you can't hold so much as a ballpoint
without tremors shooting up your hands,
battering rams against your nails,
and padlock cramps in your palms.
The last embers of that ruler
crashing into the base of your knuckles.

You do not exemplify penmanship,
I do not know the word
for someone responsible for
arranging characters and symbols,
into neat little rows and sections-
wrapping them all up snugly,
in a *Times New Roman* bow.
He who smacks black letterheads
with the elegance of a dying cow.

You cherry pick words and phrases
from the minds of better men,
forced combat,
clashing on your colosseum page.
But it isn't a page, is it?
there is no parchment involved,
no piper nor pauper to pay.
Just a blank canvas in a digital age.
No ink in a glass bottle-
with which to dip the tip
of a feathered quill in.

You do not write,
you are no writer,
you merely attach one thing to the next
they should call you a compiler.

Images from the Inside of Eden's Garden

I wish that I could tell
you that the places most
closely intertwined with "childhood"
resembled something like Eden's garden-
but in reality,
they are more akin
to warzones than they are
to biblical grandeur.

I would love to say
that the grass grows greener-
but the playgrounds are
constructed from cheap plastic
and the turf is synthetic...
and surprisingly edible.

I could tell you about
the apples coated in wax and pesticides
that line the lunch counters-
or about the snakes
who slither round the building
in the form of "parents"
who aren't on
the car pickup list.

I will tell you that
educators of any age or stage
are not merely in the business
of education-
but are rather
the first line of defense
between the loss of innocence
and both the literal and metaphorical
death of a child.

BRANCH SEVEN:

"ON GOING HOME" - (HIRAETH)

Compass

What is your path when
you possess no pattern?
When your head's a mess,
your hollow heart's a cavern?

Do you charter boats?
Do you sail the sky?
Perhaps try a cardiogram?
How about an MRI?

I found one way,
then lost it too,
I waded in dry waters,
through a litany of authors,

I found the compass
that guides the loveless.
For one with no home,
for the vagabonds that roam.

One that should work for none
but services one.
It's an affront to fears
and blockade to tears,
From the lost frontiers
of those broken years...

See,
ambition is as ambition does...
My compass points
to what is- not was.
I had a way,
then lost it too,
And I will never come running
back home to you.

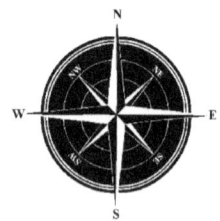

124

Earth / Heaven (Terra Haven)

Concrete backyards
chain-link fences
falling over-
North Philadelphia alleyways.

Corporeal space,
spiritual guidance,
a kind of terra haven-
an earthbound heaven
carved from practitioners
of light magic.

There I sat in an awe
of a memory-
whole and full...
grounded in your arms.

Till The Streetlamps Switched Off

Is it just me-
or do you ever notice how
when we were kids,
we always just had enough?

We always had enough energy
for whatever adventure
the new day came with-
till the streetlamps switched off.

Now we set reminders to drink water
because thirst comes secondary
to whatever task our
tired hands are completing,

and sleep always came
without the worries of tomorrow
because today was filled
with too much to even care.

I don't mean to romanticize
a time I can hardly recall-
but it just seems to me that lately-
life always gets in the way of living.

Mountain

I watched you stand upon a sudsy soapbox,
never knowing you were prone to suddenly slip.
You wore your heart on your hands-
traded blue suede for steel toed,
boisterous as ever in the citrine light.

I learned from strife what you never got the chance to teach me,
took from life what you couldn't gift me.
It was never the castles you'd breached nor the heights you reached,
neither the sands of time nor those words you'd rhyme,
but a fruit native only to your mountain's highest crest.

It's the cliffs and the spires that taught me about the liars,
those cardiac hands that demonstrated the power of firm softness,
your patient peak that took a lifetime to surmount.
Everyone's got their own mountain to climb,

and you were mine.
and you were mine.

Sharks & Minnows

Do you remember that game we'd play
on the wood paneled floors
in middle school gym class?

The one where there were "sharks"
who stood like aquatic sentries-
only until the game started, and then,
like torpedoes, explode outward
and chase down the "minnows" that
ran in desperate clusters
from one end of the undersized room
to the next.

As they swam, the scent of blood
wafted underneath your nostrils-
and you would catch them all
before they could even entertain
the thought of reaching shallow water.

Instead of running, they'd change tactics-
they would clean your scales,
whisper in your ears,
make you believe you're like them-
for they feared you
as you outgrew every tank
that they put you in.

They feared the way
your teeth looked
when you'd smile.
They put you in a cage
and got upset
when you managed to break free…

You are no minnow-
you are a fucking shark.

Tracks on 30th

I walked along the 30th street tracks
like I'd done a thousand times before...
But on a rusted bench
with a foul repugnant stench
sat a man who looked awful sore.

My bones were weary,
I had a seat,
he asked me for my lore—
we spoke, it slipped,
my latest blip, he softly said:
"tell me more."

"This isn't the theater, it's not a book,
it doesn't happen like we choose,
painted hearts and movie nights,
the white swan shaped canoes.
The jig was up,
the curtain fell,
it was all a big old ruse…"

"It happens kid, you got unlucky,
I hate to bear the news….
but guys like us,
it can be pretty rough,
cause we're just born to lose."

"Oh yea?
Why's that?
That's all there is?
Why don't we get a choice?"

"We never do,
you never will,
with that meager trailing voice…
But I can see it in you,
hear it too,
that wasn't always true…
You had one once,
what exactly did you lose?"

I had a thought
of words untaught
that materialized
and eventually caught.

This was a fractious folly,
but a black and green trolley came barreling down–
Those 30th street tracks.
I thought to myself…

"I'll never be back,
so tell him,
tell him now,
tell him what you lost… "

I told the stranger my tales of woe,
I showed the scars, from head to toe,
the tales of loss, the tales of wonder,
how I lost my hero,
my friends, my mother.

"Pretend I'm them,
pretend they're here,
say the words…
let loose…"

"I miss your faces,
the patience too,
her ever cryptic clues–
his tattered shirts,
worn out jeans,
and soleless sodden shoes.
Sometimes, now that you're gone too,
it seems like I was born to lose."

I watched the tracks,
the man got up,
he said to me:
"Just choose…"

He walked slowly
across those 30th street tracks
till his back was no longer in view.

"Don't Call Me Kid!"

"Hey kid, how are you?"
"Okay bud, take it easy."
"You're just a ki-"

You don't get to have your cake
and throw it in
someone else's face too.

You don't get to
call me an old soul,
tell me I can shoulder a world
and then treat me
as if my mind was still
in its infancy.

I have been older
than I should've been-
than I should be
since before
there was a conscious idea
of me.

So if you called me a kid
when I still was a kid-
I'd tell you that you're wrong
while holding back
the childish impulse
to bite your fucking ankle.

But if you call me "kid" now,
now that I'm "seasoned" and twenty-one,
I would be grateful,
maybe even crack a smile-
because it makes me
Feel like I'm still young.

The First Eulogy I Ever Delivered
- *a sestina of sorts*

Atop my mother's shoulder, in front of the
crowd composed of family, my first
(and unfortunately, not my last) eulogy
was recited from on high. I
spoke in a tone that could not ever
be heard but nonetheless was delivered.

A human microphone, an unfortunate first
bout with public speaking, an ever
lasting memory. There I hung, and I
(in the past tense) still delivered.
Now, I use it as the core, the
framework for every time I write a eulogy.

The view of the back wall was comforting, I
stared directly into a grand bouquet, delivered
moments ago - the most beautiful objects ever -
and looked into each petal, the
best kind of blue, sweet and sad, like a eulogy.
My mother, well, cried first.

Though I spoke, it was not I who delivered
the contents of my grandmother's eulogy.
I wonder why in the first
place a child would ever
be allowed to take the podium, but I
was promised the chance to say goodbye. The

moment was mine and would be forever.
Even though, in total, the
words, the cries, the incoherent gibberish delivered
could not really be considered a eulogy-
It was the best I could do. It was my first-
and it is something that I

Think on years later as I deliver yet another eulogy.
My fingers furl atop the podium where I
recall back, hark on an evening's moment, the
catalyst, the first and final goodbye. The first
time a real "farewell" was delivered
in the history of my ever.

132

On Going Home - (Hiraeth)

There's a kind of search that
we all undergo, fruitlessly chasing
vineyards or castles or any arbitrary venue
that doesn't ever get found.
You search for it in full buildings,
crowded places, statues, and monuments.
You look in the words
in a sea of pages...
countless books that never
say the right thing.

You look for it
in the bosoms of women
who can't pronounce your name
but are obsequious enough to distract you
from your daily routine of
sitting in a crow's nest
perched atop a watchtower.
They convince you
(by way of cheap pleasure)
that you're "living."
But you aren't. You never have.
You buy cough drops with your condoms and
let the cashier determine what brand of sick you are.
You play house with someone you hardly know
so that it feels like something called "home."

You atone for sins you didn't commit
and neglect the ones you did,
God forsaken and destitute
commending commandments for their
built-in hypocrisy as you
rattle off words like bullets without gunpowder-
the shells crashing against the floor as
they depart your shotgun lips

You've never been sold on a home
because you've never really had one...
you don't even know if it exists -
and there is no word in this
limited and ass backwards language
to possibly describe your jumbled thoughts
on going home.

4928

Simonides built a palace in his skull.
It harbored many rooms,
and wings
and halls,
and closets,
all furnished with faces
and moments
and all the varied things
that a house ought to hold.

I think in our own ways
we construct the same-
all of us like
amateur architects
piecing together all that we've lost...
hoarders of first and last breaths,
graduations, birthdays, holidays, funerals-
all stuffed into some nondescript mental venue.

Only my memory palace
has an address plastered on
the front of white paneled walls
that reads out numerically:
"4928."

When you walk up to it
there are concrete stairs
dyed red - velvet not blood -
and the railing is matte black.
Chipped paint and floral patterns
dancing their perfect dance
next to a young evergreen-
rising higher and higher
with each passing moon.

The first room is a parlor...
an old box tv,
a blue couch and chaise-
my Pop-pop sitting
not on it, but in front of it -
a big plastic cup
filled to the very brim
with Country-Time powdered iced tea.

The next is a dining room

hardly dined in,
customs shelves, a wicker basket
holding junk mail, unpaid bills,
solicitations, notices.

The kitchen is average, but narrow-
the stovetop, glass
the fridge, filled with
shoplifted Deitz & Watson.
The tile leading towards
a shoe-box backyard
marked off with an Aloe plant
trimmed so attentively by Nanny.

Up the carpeted stairs,
the first room in front of you
was a revolving door,
resident in-
resident out,
everyone had a turn in the room
where the walls cracked
and the ghosts murmured-
nobody stayed awful long...

The next room to the right,
the one my sister and I shared-
where books lined the sill,
rocking horses shook in the oncoming breeze,
and dust danced in the flickering light
from the open window.
We'd both fruitlessly try to catch
each monumentally insignificant particle.

The bathroom always has
one cabinet door
swung wide open
like a stall,
and overhead hung draping vines
and a painting
that is fuzzy and distorted
because the memory isn't as strong...
but I know we called it "Barbara."

The front room, the main room
a palace in its own right,
king sized beds,
box fans in the windows.

Ashtrays and a spilled glass of water
whose contents trickle down
the end table-
wet the ashes,
stain the floors.

I could tell you
about how the house
in my head only
smells like gravy and nicotine-
and sounds like Swan Lake and Kamahl.
How the walls and ceilings
have holes that
I don't fill on purpose.

How the home I had,
I only return to
in dreams or
a short distance-
from right across the block.

ACKNOWLEDGEMENTS

Thank you to my high school creative writing teacher, whose name I have woefully forgotten, to my English teachers, Mrs.Yakov and Mr. Wenger, and thank you to my dear friends from the class of CHS 281.

Thank you to Dr. Andrea Vinci, a professor of writing and the first person to publish me in RCSJ's "The Vanguard." The tools and encouragement you have provided me with will never be forgotten.

Thank you to my writing Professors at Rowan, Cherita Harrell and Dr. Drew Kopp, for all that you have done and taught me. Thank you as well to the professors in the English department, Dr. Hammond, Dr. Crowley, Dr. Meadowsong, Dr. Coulombe, Dr Wilcoxson, Dr. Falck, Dr. Slater, and Dr. Lomuto for all your help in the program, in classes, and all future endeavors.

Thank you to my friends and colleagues at Rowan's "Avant Literary Magazine" for publishing me (several times) and helping me with the formatting and copyediting of these poems. I may be okay with words, but you guys know syntax, and have pushed to both "do" and "be" better in all of my varied literary endeavors. Thank you specifically to Adam, Jack, Meg, Steven, Peter, Sam, Mia-Sara, Cecilia, and everyone who attends.

Thank you to Rowan's Poetic Justice, Kiara, Jaylen, Rey, Danih, and everyone there who gave me courage and validation when it comes to poetry.

Thank you to Alyssa for the design of the cover and interior format of this book. I would not have been able to do this without you.

Thank you to the editors and production behind "Calliope: A Poetry Podcast " for giving me the chance to perform my poem "Old Fashioned" for your podcast and the subsequent interview – it's very cool to find yourself on Spotify. Thank you to Thom, Eric, Nyds, Nick, Hannah, Rach, Tara, and Rob. You all do an amazing job and I am so grateful.

Thank you to Larry Robin and the team at Moonstone Press for including me and my work in three of your printed anthologies - specifically 'Snowy Evenings," "Dogwood," and "Amythest

Atmosphere." You are a beacon of Philadelphia publication, and the world could learn a thing or two from you fine people.

Thank you to my high school, college, work, and other such friends made along the way, who have gotten me through some of my worst moments, and will continue to be friends for life- you all mean more than I have the time to tell you, but just know how much I love and appreciate you: Austin, Teagan, Gabe M, Alan, Brandon, Benjamin, Abby, Chris, Nataly, Rion, Alex, Jason N, Logan, Tommy, Drew, Mike, Ray, Peter, Julie, Danny, Donovan, and John and all of you who have shared a smile or a laugh with me.

Thank you to my chosen family from around the world, Ian, Gabe C, Max, Dimitri, Alix, Hunter, Ben, Joe, Cameron, Louis, Henderson, Sean, Jayden, Michael, Ryan, Preston, and Wayne - who we lost tragically, but miss dearly every day.

Thank you to my Uncle Jim, who has cared for me and taught me so much, even when he had no obligation to do so. You're a good man and a shining example of how to stay young in a world that does its best to age you so quickly.

Thank you to my Uncle Ron, who even though I get upset with, or wonder where certain sentences come from, I love you and respect everything you have fought for and against – you are one of my heroes. And to my Aunt Vanessa, who is a shining light that my uncle and my family has been so fortunate to see, it is an honor to call you family.

Thank you to my cousin Jeff, who gave me purpose and reassurance in some of my lowest moments. We see eye to eye-on many things, and it has been a joy to know and be a part of your life. And thank you Erica, for being right there next to Jeff in all of the support you have given me. Thank you, Stephen, for always lending a joke or some levity in tough times – though you are and always will be more than the court jester.

Thank you to my Aunt Phyllis, Titi Janet, and her wonderful kids and my adopted siblings Janely & Angel. Though we do not-directly share our biology, you are more "family" to me than most of those who share my D.N.A. I love you all so much.

Thank you to my brothers Gabriel D and Saul, who I hope nothing but the best for, and hope to see more often in our future. And to my Mum-Mum Lana, who I miss every day.

Thank you to my father, Thomas, who could not take a compliment if his life depended on it. You have shown me the kind of strength that few men would be able to replicate, and you mean to me more than I have the courage to say to your face – maybe we're just socially awkward. I love you Dad, always.

Thank you to my amazing younger sister Lizzy, who I am so proud of. You, more than being a sibling, are one of my closest friends, and have been with me since the very beginning. I love you, and I will always be there for you- even when we inevitably live on opposite ends of the country.

Thank you to my beautiful, smart, incredible partner Jayna, who all of this is large-in-part for. You are my beacon, my inspiration, my star, my light at the end of the tunnel that I have waited many years to find. I wish there were stronger words than "I love you," but I'll be working on finding them... and I'll get back to you. And to Jen and Scott, who have opened their home so graciously to me. I appreciate and love you both.

Thank you to my Pop-pop, long passed, for being my litmus test for many things in life. You taught me the patience that took you a lifetime to cultivate and fostered in me a love of creativity and purple elephants. I will never work a day in my life since you taught me to do what I love. And to my Nanny, who I miss every time I pick up a superman comic or read the journals she left for me that inspired several of these poems. I love you and miss you both more than words can say.

Thank you to my Tidsy, who without her help, this book would never have been able to have ever been written in the first place. I owe you a debt I can never repay, though I'm sure you'd say something like "just do your best, and that's repayment enough-" so here it is. You have taught me more I am able to bring to the forefront at any given moment, but these lessons will last me a lifetime, and grateful is too small a word to use to describe in the context of you... so I'll get back to you when I find a more apt one. I love you to the moon and back.

And lastly, thank you to my mother, who sowed the seeds of a dream in me, and who I hope to inspire to put her own work out into the world. We're all waiting patiently for you, whenever you are ready. The truth is I could write an entire essay in your honor, but you'll have to settle for this book instead. I'll love you forever, and like you for always.

AUTHOR'S NOTE

The interesting truth about this collection is that never in my wildest dreams would I have considered publishing them. I always preferred to watch or let other people do the talking, the writing, the living, and as I grew up the view from the sideline became all the more comfortable with each passing day. But as many of you know, being a bystander to your own existence does not lead to memorable moments. At that point, you may as well just live in front of a cell-phone, or a book, or a television - though I make ample time for those as well. This collection of poetry consists of one-hundred-and-fourteen poems that were written from the age of seventeen to the present (as of writing, that would be twenty-one.) My writing journey did not begin in the typical scholarly fashion - I did not journal, nor doodle, nor write "dear diary" every other day to jot down whatever childlike endeavor I had undergone. It began in the form of reading, and as soon as I could, I leap-frogged from the "learn your ABC's" children's books to the good stuff - Jules Verne, Robert Frost, Stephen Crane, and King, T.S Elliot, Angelou, Byron, Keats, Shelley, Shel Silverstein - the list goes on and on and on… I firmly believe that we as people are doomed to copy one another, be that from art, to our very mannerisms and piths of our personalities- but the goal is to be less of a continuation of our predecessors, and more or less an upgrade. I do not have the arrogance to deem myself better than anyone on that list, in fact at this point I feel almost like an imitation, and an amateur to boot (which is quite evident in the writings from my younger years, but in order to tell that story... they have to be here. And as far as I'm concerned, every piece is equally as relevant to that mission) but that is the nature of imposter syndrome sprinkled with a seasoning of pessimism, and so I will simply let the work do the talking, and hope that I have paid homage to the wonderful figures who have influenced my life… be that family, or authors, or Disney cartoons, or whatever moment in time sparked the writing of these poems. "A Walk in His Woods" is a book that parallels my whole entire life. My nickname from my friends has always been "Tree," and in teaching children they have adopted that with the moniker "Mr. Tree," because Mr. DeMarco felt too stuffy and out of place. There is also the thematic importance there, as growth and this whole "coming of age" nonsense sort of weave their ways together quite naturally, but these are part of
meanings that we conjure up for any multitude of reasons - though at this moment, they serve me rather well.

The writing done here is broken up into seven branches (or you can call them chapters) to encompass an aspect of my life or writing that seemed to fit. "Arboretum" covers my experimentation with Naturalism and transcendental writing, like Whitman and Dickinson first did - as well as trying to infuse some modernism in there along with urban life and anecdotal experience. "Dedicated Dedications" is compiled for people who I wanted to say something to, or for, or pay homage to in the form of an ode or a Golden Shovel poem (Sidebar: Golden Shovel being the form of poetry first penned by Terrance Hayes in 2010 with his poem "Golden Shovel" after a Gwen Brooks poem "We real cool" that takes the source poem and uses a segment as the final word of each line in the new one.) I find that form allows for some flexibility- a way to pay tribute to the words and works that embed themselves in our heads and hearts and make a meaningful change, and then to channel that, and create a conversation and degree of inter-textuality. For me, really, it is one of the highest expressions of love. "All That Falls - Between the Cracks" is quite literally the miscellaneous section of the collection, the vagabonds of my work so to speak - but is still home to some poems that are near and dear to me , including "Anchor," the first poem I had ever written (and published later on in college) in my high school creative writing class. "Love & Idiosyncrasies" is rather self-explanatory, as I am not someone who has had a great deal of luck in that department, but have felt it so deeply, and channeled it into my writing. "Born Forty" encompasses the feeling of being older in your mind than you are in body - this is a consequence of maturity and parentification, though perhaps is just relative to the rampant immaturity amongst fellow members of my generation. "Pledges & Oubliettes" is a section dedicated to words and the pitfalls that come with them, speaking, writing, being some way and doing things in our world come with a set of labels and expectations. It's rather vague, but that is simply the nature of ontology. "On Going Home (Hiraeth) comes from a Welsh word that describes a feeling akin to homesickness, a kind of longing with added caveat of uncertainty for what you're longing for. I've never really felt at home in my life, so I'm not sure what I'm missing, but I miss it nonetheless, and that is the pith of the chapter.

Ultimately, I cannot fully express in words the depth of feeling that I experience in this world, be them from school, work, the daily minutia, anything really - but poetry has been an outlet for that - to try and convert into language, to give a shape to emotion, to feeling, to being, and this collection has been my attempt at doing something relatively close. I'm not trying to reinvent the wheel, nor etch out a spot in history with the delusions of potential immortality, I just have one thing that I want to do… In a world that is so hell bent on destroying itself, the only real combatant is creation, and thus comes expressions and endeavors like these. Thank you for being a part of that, genuinely, thank you.

- Dimitrius Alexander DeMarco

www.ingramcontent.com/pod-product-compliance
Lightning Source LLC
Chambersburg PA
CBHW061802120626
46550CB00005B/2106

* 9 7 9 8 2 1 8 7 1 7 5 7 5 *